FIRST YEARS IN EUROPE.

FIRST YEARS IN EUROPE.

BY

GEORGE H. CALVERT,

AUTHOR OF "SCENES AND THOUGHTS IN EUROPE," "THE GENTLEMAN," ETC.

BOSTON:
WILLIAM V. SPENCER.
1866.

Presswork by John Wilson and Son.

PREFACE.

IN 1856 were published, in *Putnam's Magazine*, two papers entitled, "Weimar in 1825," and "Goettingen in 1824." The acceptance they found, together with the studious enjoyment the writer had in registering the scenes and doings of a sunny long-past time, led him, some years later, to continue and complete reminiscences of a first residence in Europe.

With the most resolute will, it is as impossible, in a volume with the title and contents of this, to suppress an autobiographical tint as it were to stifle the odor of ignited tobacco. The significance of incidents, the liveliness of scenes, the pertinence of reflections, so often depend on the individual agent, that to attempt to efface or conceal his personality were as abortive as to try without thread to hold together a necklace of beads, be they of glass or of pearls. The writer must be behind every sentence; and as he is not, like the bead-string, dead and passive, but is a living active soul, he cannot be kept always out of sight. Too strenuous an effort so to keep him would take the color out of many a page. The author will be glad if the reader shall find this apology superfluous.

The slight record of kindnesses received forty years ago invades no sanctities or sensibilities, and no apology is offered for giving the names of those who rendered them, several of whom are still living.

NEWPORT, R. I., *August*, 1866.

CONTENTS.

		PAGE
I.	From New York to Antwerp	9
II.	Antwerp	23
III.	Antwerp. — The Cathedral	36
IV.	Antwerp. — The Museum	49
V.	From Antwerp to Goettingen	64
VI.	Goettingen	86
VII.	My First Vacation	127
VIII.	Weimer	165
IX.	From Goettingen to Antwerp	199
X.	From Antwerp to Edinburgh	220
XI.	Edinburgh	244
XII.	From Edinburgh to Paris	278

FIRST YEARS IN EUROPE.

I.

FROM NEW YORK TO ANTWERP.

REJOICING to escape from the roll and vastness of the sea, we were embraced on the seventh day by the hills and green fields that help to make the harbor of Halifax. It was my first voyage, and my first sight of a foreign land. On the 16th of August, 1823, the *Francis Freeling* cast anchor in front of the town. Immediately a barge came off to convey the British Minister and his secretary to the Governor's. The *Francis Freeling* — an armed brig of about three hundred tons, one of the British royal packets that plied monthly between New York and Falmouth, by way of Halifax — having been taken for himself and suite by Mr. Stratford Canning, then Minister to the United States, about to return home, he had kindly proposed to my father, that on my way toward Goettingen I should accompany him to England.

In the afternoon came to me from the Governor

of Nova Scotia, Lieutenant-General Sir James Kempt, an invitation to dinner at six for the next day, Sunday; and on Sunday the invitation was repeated for Monday. The Governor's large round dinner-table, lighted from the centre of the ceiling, with its fifteen or sixteen guests, is the most vivid of my Nova Scotian memories. On one day I had beside me Judge Haliburton, since temporarily famous as "Sam Slick;" on the other, a Colonel who had lost a leg and an arm at Waterloo. As to the conversation, in that I was, on both days, the most important member of the company. Did I regale this circle of royalists — all subjects, and most of them highly-trusted servants, of a King — with a sonorous laudation of democracy, flanked by a dogmatic argumentation, with running expository accompaniment, on our federative system: — I had lately been studying the "Federalist," and in my junior year at Harvard had taken a prize for declamation: — or, was I, fresh from the principal seat of learning in New England, so virulently inoculated with interrogation, that, not to miss the golden opportunity before me, goaded too by the appetite for knowledge possessed by every competent gentleman just launched on his travels, I plied the whole circle, individually and collectively, with questions? Either of these solutions of my importance presupposes "Young America" in turgescent, licentious vivaciousness; whereas in 1823 that unblushing prematurity was yet in swaddling-clothes. But let the reader figure to himself, on a clear August afternoon of this present 1862, the chief dignitaries of Halifax, civil and military, converging towards the Governor's drawing-room, while, with piston-punctuality, the *Europa* or the *Africa* glides into the harbor, and a few minutes after, the Governor and his assembled guests greet Lord Lyons, fresh from Washington, attended by his secretary, but unattended by a young American friend. What the purport and tone would be of the liveliest talk at the dinner-table, may be securely inferred from the comments, for the past year, of British journals, quarterly, monthly, weekly, daily, and of British public speakers, parliamentary and ministerial, on American affairs. True, 1823 was not loaded with a momentous world-watched conflict; but the spirit in which this tremendous war is viewed by the governing classes of England is the growth of many decades. The breaths of English opinion and feeling, expired toward the United States since 1810, are the wind from whose sowing is reaped the present whirlwind of English rancor and denunciation. The harvest is not yet over: there may be another, and another kind of whirlwind to be reaped hereafter.[1]

1 Written in 1862, these sentences embody the feeling of that anxious period. With the triumphant vindication of American

It will thus be perceived what a potent, though negative, sway was wielded over the company by its youthful, silent, American member; and how, especially, the derisive tongue of the inchoate "Sam Slick," was probably bridled by the imperative proprieties of hospitality.

On the nineteenth of August the *Francis Freeling*, Captain Cunningham, weighed anchor.

Who has not seen the setting sun swallowed day after day by the sea; has not watched the stars swaying through the heavens and dancing to and fro to the rhythm of the up-heaved billows; has not felt an awe, tempered by delight, as the stout ship beneath him poises herself an instant on the writhing wind-whipped waves, and then darts forward with victorious speed, bravely obedient to the mastering will at the helm; has not had the magnificent monotony of smooth days broken by a

national unity have subsided the excitement and the uncertainties of a fearful civil conflict; while by the results of the conflict the mutual attitude of the United States and England is different from what it has at any time been since our existence as a nation. Not from England only, but from all Europe, we have won a full recognition of our republican sufficiency, and between England and the United States the tone of feeling on both sides is at this moment healthier than ever before. May the great mother and the great daughter henceforth stand side by side interlocked in the twofold embrace of Commerce and Letters. United, they may predominate over Christendom for the good of mankind. War between them were one of the worst calamities that could befall human advancement.

June, 1866.

storm that comes bellowing out of immensities, right at his frail bark, and, shut in from the protecting stars between the close-driving clouds and the uprisen waters, has not been thrilled by a sublime terror at his helplessness, and then by a sublime sense of power, as the solitary hunted ship leaps through the tempest to turn out her wet canvas to the morrow's sun; whoso has not traversed an ocean, quickened by its majestic lessons, has missed an invigorating chapter in the contents of a human life. The sea is a continuous sublimity, and the spirit of him who can assimilate its wonders and its grandeurs, it braces for the struggles of the land.

On deck you have the expansions of a voyage; below deck its limitations. The present generation travel between America and Europe in steam-palaces of three thousand tons; and still they find themselves "cabined and confined" below. With how much narrower a radius must then have been drawn our circumscriptions in a brig of three hundred tons. The cabin had but half its complement of passengers, and at the table which would have been full with eight, we counted, with the Captain and Doctor, five.

The Captain, a man of about fifty, of middle height and thin, with Roman features, a Lieutenant in the Royal Navy, and lame from a wound received in the War of 1812, had been carried prisoner into one of our Southern ports, where the kindness bestowed upon him, which he cordially acknowledged, assuaged somewhat in him the anti-American animosity prevalent among his class.

The Doctor was a medium-sized man under thirty, with a dull eye, and one of those turbid complexions that soap will not clarify. Luckily for me, probably, I gave him no opportunity of proving his skill; but he gave me one for a retort: for, pronouncing, one day at dinner, a sweeping judgment upon the people of New York, as being low and ill-bred, I rejoined, that a foreigner in a strange city would be apt to form his opinion of its inhabitants by the company he kept.

Our little brig did her task well; and late on Monday afternoon the eighth of September, with just light enough to see her way, she entered the harbor of Falmouth.

That young men, who from the law of youth have little power of judgment, should yet be so ready with decisions, must proceed from a necessity of nature, that things that are to be big must not only first be little, but must assert themselves in their unconscious littleness. Thence, men who are to come to a rich ripeness, signalize their entrance into manhood with the uttering of crudities. Many joyous blossoms miss the happiness of fruitage; but fruit there were none without blossoms. These intellectual tadpoles will often be found wriggling vivaciously in youthful diaries. Nor have I on this score any complaint against mine; but now that it is dragged from its long obscurity, I cannot help wishing that it were likewise fuller, not of facts — for many a fact, involving, as every one does, a relation between at least two things, demands for its accurate report hardly less practised maturity than do thoughtful judgments — but of transcripts, brief as may be, of words heard or things seen, especially in motion; for these give an everlasting liveliness to journals, even to those of men in whom the shapeless embryos of the intellect have long since been wrought into compactness and symmetry by time and its exercitations.

Three hundred miles in an English mail-coach is become a privileged reminiscence. Falmouth, which is now six or seven hours distant from London, was forty in 1823. "Mules carrying copper on pack-saddles; women neat and often pretty; coachmen sober; hedges unclipt; Dorset County barren; Exeter Cathedral, finer than Westminster Abbey." This last comment proves that the diary was written out after my arrival in London. Unhappily there is not a word about fellow-passengers, or what they said. At six o'clock on Thursday morning, the eleventh, I found myself at the Spring Garden Coffee-House, Charing-Cross; and after an early breakfast sallied forth into the Strand.

A youngster, fresh from Yorkshire, has not a more absolute title upon London than one from the Banks of the Hudson or the Potomac, the national alienation giving even a keener edge to the zest wherewith the American enters upon his property. The Tower is his, and the Thames, and he walks into Westminster Abbey with filial reverence. He is like a wealthy heir, sent from home a bantling, come back at twenty-one to take possession. He runs about, refreshing and verifying and rectifying his vague memories. His rights are so deep that they are inalienable; for they descend to him through the books he has read, and the plays he has seen, and the history he has learnt, and the language he speaks, and the prayers he breathes, and the imaginations he has fondled.

Being yet only a traveller incidentally, London was but a station on my road to Goettingen. Of the few days I spent so busily my most cordial reminiscence is a dinner to which I accompanied Mr. Canning at his sister's, where was the Under-Secretary of State, Mr. Planta, and where was to have been the principal Secretary, Mr. George Canning. But he was detained by business; and so I failed to bring away from Europe the visual and auricular image of one of England's most celebrated latter statesmen. Mr. Stratford Canning, whose kindness to me I ever have pleasure in remembering, has since, for his eminent diplomatic services, been raised to the peerage under the title of Lord Stratford de Redcliffe.

On Saturday morning the twentieth of September, having embarked at the Custom House on the steamboat *Talbot*, I passed down the Thames, and reaching Ostend at midnight, set out by *diligence* on Sunday for Ghent. Now for the first time I felt myself in a foreign land, the foreignness assailing me unceasingly through eye and ear. In the diary of my first day on the Continent I find a few words, that are not the effusion of an immature judgment, but to which even a greater significance is imparted by the youthfulness of the observer. They are these, — "The inhabitants have a sad look." One battered by the world, who knows, from having braved, its hardships and its woes, would not so readily note and comment on, or at least would not be startled by, what to him would seem almost a thing of course. But to a young man, whose own heart and face have not yet been shadowed by the oppressions and glooms of life, the sad look of a whole people, when first beheld, wears a dim terrible mysteriousness. If he be a man of sensibility, he will be affected as by a suddenly confronted, sorrowful phantom. And there it is still to-day that look, transmitted from generation to generation, — a dreary look as of helpless orphanage, stamped on the countenance by the worn and wearied soul; a never-ending eclipse, darkening the life of the multitude with the opaque bulk of ever-revolving never-absent poverty; that fixed, silent, mournful look, the token of a heart-graven despair, as if the animal spirits were ever attending the funeral of the hopes and the aspirations, — there it is, stretching across Northern Europe into Asia, giving a ghastly aspect to the peoples, that pallor of the spirit and the visage, the badge of inherited impoverishment and lifelong destitution.

The human countenance elsewhere, whether seen singly or in crowds, does not always glisten with the radiance whereof it is capable; and a Lavater going up Broadway at about nine o'clock in the morning, when the workers in Wall Street are streaming down, with their faces full of the coming day, would surely not be impressed with the nobleness of man's physiognomy. Yet there he would find in it any thing but deadness or apathy. Besides the evidence of a good breakfast that it furnishes, it is alive with intellect and feeling and hope. The intellect is somewhat arithmetical; the feeling may be sympathy for the contents of a neighbor's pocket; the hopes are belike *bearish;* but they give life to the face, and open vistas in it, however these may end in gilded upholstery and a numerous table fragrant with French cookery.

The face of the European peasantry opens no vistas: it is sodden in gloom. Let any one, who would verify for himself their condition, loiter in a small rural town of Belgium, or among the field-laborers in Germany, or peer into the minutiæ of agricultural or manufacturing statistics, or listen to the report of some who have been met fleeing their fatherland, to escape the daily disheartening sight of widespread want and hopeless misery.

For me, in those unshadowed years, enough on that first continental day were the outsides of things, all new and strange, — the huge *diligence*, with its three compartments and its three horses abreast; the strange tongue; the little boys on the road-side, standing on their heads, as the best attitude for begging; the many cottages; the populousness; the garden-like tillage; the straight roads; the fenceless, hedgeless, weedless fields. The mere stowing away of new images, like packing parcels into a carpet-bag, expands the mind that is expansible. Indeed, in this stowing, if done at the right time, in the right way, with the right parcels, consists all of education, the secret of which is, to apportion the material supplied from without to the inward power of assimilation, — the food to the feeder, so that all be cleanly absorbed; and then the mental limbs dilate and ripen, each up to the rim of its capacity. But a traveller, still more a young one, needs companionship, — a friendly, not to say a confidential, comrade. The new parcels are better handled by four hands than by two; more are stowed away and in better condition; for in all human doings there is no enlivener like sympathy. Loneliness weighs nowhere with a more gloomy gravity than on a young man journeying in a strange land. He is in an unwalled prison under the open sky. For me a friendly station was near at hand.

At our steady pace of five miles an hour, over the straight, paved, trembling, clattering road, we reached Ghent at four, and started the next morning at four; my seat, a commanding one, being on the outside behind. For partner in elevation I had a Swede, a merchant or mercantile agent. He was one of those men who live loosely on the surface of the world, unsteadied in his place by the moral roots which give to life its higher worth and dignity.

We have all heard of the sty of Epicurus; but the philosopher himself did not live in it. He was a clean refined gentleman of purest life. Through individual organization *his* pleasure was drawn exclusively from virtuous practices; and no doubt the surprise on finding himself alive after the death of his body, turned into delight on discovering that in the life after the earth-life there is wider scope for the enjoyment of pure desires. But his doctrine of pleasure, which wrought upward in one so finely and exceptionally organized as he was, works downward and issues in sensualism, when wielded by animal natures; and were it not that so many mortals would have been Epicureans, gross or delicate, had no Epicurus ever lived, he might for these two thousand years in his higher abodes, have undergone pangs of conscience at the continued and countless multiplication of Epicurean litters; perceiving that even after centuries of Christian reign, not only is Christendom thickly sprinkled with disbelievers in a life beyond the grave, but that some of his (Epicurus's) sleekest pigs are to be seen occasionally in Christian pulpits. As to my Swedish neighbor, he was a cleanly, civil pig, of about forty, well-grown, with a fresh healthy complexion, whose bodily comforts and enjoyments were not allowanced by dutiful scruples.

To the contagion of Epicureans, of coarser or finer grain, the young man who goes forth into the world is exposed, as he is to malaria and shipwreck. Had the *diligence* upset, the loftiness of my seat, which gave me so good a view of Flanders, might have brought dislocation of limb or neck; but the *diligence* did not upset, nor did I suffer any moral dislocation from contact with the Swede, whose figure and talk are more vivid to me to-day that I am recording them, than they have ever been at any other moment since we descended together from our unwieldly vehicle, when it halted on the banks of the Schelde.

Toward eight o'clock the endless vista of the straight, broad, tree-flanked road began to be dimly closed. Soon the vague outline took more definite shape. "What is that?" — "The Cathedral of Antwerp," answered the Swede. The words knocked familiarly at my heart. 'T was the sudden apparition of an early friend. My mother had often told us children of having gone, when a child, with her parents up into the spire of the cathedral to witness a far-off battle, in which the French were victorious, — a result not welcome to the party she was with. That battle was of some moment to me; for, had it issued otherwise than it did, I should not have been here to speak of it, as in that case my maternal grandfather would not have emigrated from Belgium to America, which he did with all his family about the year 1794.

There it was, that great spire, with my mother in it, growing taller and livelier as mile after mile we neared the city; until we came to the river-bank, when it towered up so close and palpable, that it seemed within a stone's throw of us, piercing and adorning the heavens with its attenuating beauty, one of the marvels of Europe and glories of architectural art. At nine I got into the *Hotel d'Angleterre*, and at ten went out to find my uncle.

II.

Antwerp.

MAN'S business — did he but know it — is, to learn, ever to learn, never to cease learning; which business the young carry on only more briskly, learning unconsciously even more than consciously. Passively or semi-passively they absorb knowledge, — as growing leaves their sustenance from air, — silently receiving, in periods of seeming inaction, images, and impressions which are to be aliment for the opinions and convictions of later years. In the transition from an American college to a German university there intervened a long suspension of active book-work. Before entering on more manly studies I was pasturing untethered in fields rich with novelties, — sprightly, indulgent preceptors, demanding no effort in their pupil.

I found myself domesticated in an old *chateau*, six miles from Antwerp, surrounded with a moat, filled by the tide of the distant Schelde. There was no longer a draw to the bridge, but at the end of it a heavy iron-clamped portal let you into an open quadrangular court, around which rose the walls, enclosing a roomy, commodious mansion, with a small chapel in one of the towers. Beyond the moat, on all sides were trees, more or less thickly planted, with a view in part to landscape effects. In one direction, just beyond the trees, was a spacious garden; in another, not half a mile distant, a small village, where dwelt the peasants to whom the land was leased. Outside the moat, on the east, ran a straight country road, thickly shaded by trees.

It is an easy life,. to saunter down the slope of idleness, plucking flowers that you have not planted; but if you follow it too far the slope grows barren and steep, to plunge soon into an abyss. Indeed, only at the top, where idleness is temporary relaxation, is it enjoyment; and healthy life instinctively rejects it as a foe. My idleness was made busy by the multifarious novelty about me. There were dinner-parties, small and large, where cheerfulness was provided by intimacy, and refinement and elegance by long social culture and the mingling of the sexes, and where the *cuisine* (as I discovered in later more gustatory years) was most appetizing and delicate. And there was a ball at another *chateau*, where I was in the midst of numerous kin, of all ages and degrees, running into the dilutions of fourth and fifth cousinship.

In face of the protest of Nature, emphasized by

ever-recurring cases of physical and mental debility, — exhibited often in idiotism and lunacy, — pride of birth, and the calculations of thrift, and the fervors of affection, have led to much intermarriage among near kindred, not only in monarchic, oligarchic Europe, where tradition and statute have maintained a privileged class, but in republican America, where, there being no such class, that which holds a social preëminence is far more freely replenished and re-invigorated from the general reservoir than in Europe.

In a wealthy provincial continental city, — when it is not a modern accretion of manufacture, or commerce, — the upper class, socially speaking, is made up of a *noblesse*, titled or untitled, who in Belgium formed so exclusive and isolated a body — or rather series of bodies — that between two neighboring towns, like Antwerp and Ghent for instance, no bonds are knit through marriage or personal intimacy, or even acquaintanceship; and within each city's own precincts, merchants and members of the professions of law or medicine are not members of this social corporation, nor even the clergy, they being drawn almost entirely from the *bourgeoisie* and peasantry.

Sidney Smith said, "It takes a million of people to make a good society." If civilized humanity has so little fine juice as to need a million to impart to the extract called "society" the quality, quantity, variety required to give it body, flavor, and pungency, what must be the result of a distilment out of eighty or a hundred thousand, and from a population where intellectual culture is meagre and partial, and where there are no scholars, and few books, and fewer readers. In such a community a cultivated man would starve; for he must have books for himself, and the effect of books on others, to create an atmosphere wherein he can breathe growingly.

The disease of a practical materialism prevails, wherever on the globe gold has been able to make itself into heaps; as though by the friction and jingle incident to the piling of coin of this metal were generated a miasma that strikes right into the heart of mankind. In a Belgian city, whose highest class — highest by wealth, by inherited title, by acknowledged position — is self-isolated, with the ordinary outlets choked up by individual apathy, aggravated by the insignificancy of a small State, and with the contractions of a purely Romish education and surroundings — in such a city, whose upper circle buries itself in itself, this saffron disease, this moral jaundice is, through the stagnation of the social atmosphere, petted into chronic obstinacy and fatality.

By the growth of population, the growth of wealth, the growth of ideas, and the diffusion of knowledge, the nobility as a governing class has been in the most advanced countries of continental Europe virtually superseded. The State, in all its functions, civil and military, can now be, and is, administered without the predominance of privileged classes. Hence these for the most part retreat into an Epicurean paradise of the senses, lying on a secluded, undisputed social preëminence; and as, to maintain this elevation — especially with the modern encroachments of money-reaping industry — cash is a first necessity, a condition indivisible from the efficiency of blood, much of the steel that formerly sparkled in knightly spurs and gleamed in sabres, is now diverted into strong-boxes and carving-knives.

Belgium is utterly Catholic. In a population of four millions and a half are counted but a few thousand Protestants. There is no enforcement; people may be what they please. Annually an official visits the monasteries and nunneries, and, throwing open the doors, proclaims that all and any one may go out. But no one goes out. And no one goes, nor has gone for nearly three centuries, out of the Church. What of heresy the heel of Alva could not crush, nor his sword and axe hew away, was torn out piecemeal by the pincers of the pious Inquisitors, Torquemada and his deputy, Titelmann. In those terrible years of the sixteenth century the protesting element in this people was cauterized almost unto death. It was not persecution that then raged in Flanders and Brabant; it was deracination, annihilation. The Flemings were, for many generations after, the best of Catholics, unquestioning, submissive to the Church. Latterly, their innate love of freedom is making for itself religious vents; and jealousy of ecclesiastical power, and resistance to priestly abuse, have become an element, and a most wholesome, enlivening element, in Belgian life.

Liberal thinkers, men whose own minds are kept ever hospitably open to new thought, are puzzled and startled by the great fact, that the lines drawn on the map of Europe at the epoch of the Reformation in the sixteenth century between Catholicism and Protestantism have remained fixed ever since. In these three centuries Protestantism has made no territorial gains. The fact looks formidable and discouraging, even mysterious. But consider the guards and influences around a Catholic to keep him Catholic. The family-power, which, immeasurably strengthened since the Reformation by jealousy of extraneous hostile religious insinuation, works hourly from infancy into manhood; the force of custom on natures kept watchfully under the stroke of its unresting tilt-hammers; seclusion, in part voluntary, with its negative might; the ban upon the Bible and all books unstamped by the Church; the threats and cajolements of priests, each one, in the mind of the believer, invested with a divine power of binding and loosing the soul, — a very warden of the world to come; the hold thus obtained over the imagination, made to move for its safety, like wild geese behind their leader, in the wake of the Church; the dread of change in the timid, and the trouble of change to the indolent, and the unreasonableness of change to the unreasoning; the mountain of ignorance, pressing ever downward; — here is circumvallation within circumvallation of fences, fosses, walls, to guard each Catholic fold, and every member of each, against the foxes and wolves and vipers of heresy. Add to this as supplementary safeguards, where there is exposure to contact with heretics, the pride of creed and the slowness of reason; and one can understand, without despondency, why the lines of Protestantism have not been pushed forward in Europe. But although the geographical boundaries have not changed, they have been countlessly overleapt, and the victories of Protestantism, with its freer thinking, its freer speaking, its freer printing, have been, though noiseless, so decisive and so universal, that Catholicism is not at all what it was in the sixteenth century, even in its strong holds; so that the priesthood everywhere, even in Italy and Spain, has been obliged to bend virtually (though nominally never yielding) before the majestic advance of human thought, impelled and inspired by the human conscience. Let not the progressive and the spiritually-minded despair; the world of mind moves, moves ever forward towards clearer day, even as the earth moves in the stillest, darkest night.

I had not been a fortnight in Antwerp when there fell on me a shadow; or, rather, rays that had descended with all the cheeriness of a May morning, grew of a sudden wintry,— the rays that radiate from that central sun of the talking world, Opinion. It was whispered about that I was a Protestant. How the lurid suspicion originated I never learnt. I had said no word about the matter to any one. Probably on going to mass with my uncle at the cathedral, — my first entrance into a Catholic church, — he had observed a crudeness in my bearing, confirmatory of vague rumors that may have come across the ocean respecting my mother. What a shower of sentimental darts were flying at unconscious me. With what purgatorial faces, in what defeated tones, was the suspicion passed round, when were gathered together three or four feminine commentators. Doubt as to so fearful a psychological calamity could not be long endured. One day I was accosted in a shop by one of the matronly social summities, a lady whose piety was too strong for aristocratic *morgue;* for hers was almost the only table where a priest was ever met. She put the question bluntly to me: I answered her as directly; and thus the matter of fact was firmly settled. Whatever Catholics may believe of us, we Protestants allow that Catholics are Christians, or may be, as well as we, who seldom make the most of our Protestant vantage-ground. On hearing my admission, the pious interrogator showed her Christianity, by keeping out of her countenance, from tenderness to my feelings, the whole horror of her heart.

Plenty of good men are good Catholics. Catholicism suits for the present their organization. They have been brought up to it, and feel no inward want unsatisfied. I admit the fitness of their being Catholic, and I cordially accord to them the respect that man owes to man, — nay, they have from me even a brotherly sympathy. There are Catholics who are men of fine intellect ana high culture; but if such are broad and genial and true, they are tolerant, partially tolerant, — and in so far un-Romish; and their tolerance of heresy is tolerated by the Church only because she can no longer, even against her own children, rigidly enforce her arrogant exclusive assumption, with its ferocious anathemas, its unhuman maledictions on heretics.

For me, as for so many, it is a need of my being to think for myself; and the more important the subject the more imperious the need. I could as soon engage a man to frame opinions for me on any great life-question, especially one involving sentiment, — and religion involves the highest, — as I could employ him to digest my dinner, or aerate *my* blood with *his* lungs. Had I therefore been brought up a Catholic I should not have continued such; but the early influences about me would have been much different from what they were ; not so congenial, and more or less debilitating, retarding and sophisticating. Thence I thank my excellent mother — and how often have I thanked her — that she, by her upright clear-mindedness, put me at once, from my early childhood, into a freer atmosphere. Transplanted from Belgium to Maryland, she found herself in one, and she had the largeness to be braced by its strength. Among her new liberties was that of the Bible, — hitherto a sealed book. Simply from reading the New Testament she became a Protestant.

We are accustomed to speak of the tenderness and care and watchful nurture whereof through all the hours of long years we have been the objects, as the source of our inexpressible filial obligation, as the great cause of gratitude to our parents ; but infinitely, unspeakably more — a debt that is not to be weighed or measured — than as the protectors of our being do we owe them as its authors, as those through whom we have this eternal gift of life, this daily repeated unending miracle of being, with its refulgent worlds of thought and sensation. These worlds being vast and luminous, according primarily to our endowments, and then secondarily to the freedom and culture given to these, I have cause for especial thankfulness to my mother, that she, with throes of spirit, — and they were probably long and lacerating, — emancipated herself, and thus her children, from inherited bondage to priesthood. She joined the Protestant Episcopal Church, having come into it through exercise of the great fundamental Protestant right of independent private judgment. In her liberation she was not aided by any clergyman; and after the victory gained by her own mental energies, had any attempted, under other names and forms, to lay again on her the hand of ecclesiastical authority, he would have found that the soul that in quitting the Catholic communion had asserted its divine right, and its might to shatter creeds, was ready to reassert them to repel all priestly assumption.

From vices incident to, inherent in all priesthoods,—spiritual pride and love of the temporalities of power and place, — the clergy of most Protestant sects are ever striving to confiscate for their own behoof this essential peerless right of private judgment, which is at once the corner-stone and keystone of all Protestantism. They, too, will be trying to lay sacrilegious hands on the divine holiness within each human breast, — the conscience.

They, too, like a religious passiveness in their flocks. They like to have them placid, dependent sheep, who will not attempt to jump the ecclesiastical pen. They do not use creeds and formularies as temporary fences and breastworks behind which the better to defend for a while the citadels of religious truth ; but too often as chains and tethers, which limit and distort that truth. In their egotistic exaggeration of the priestly office they so magnify themselves, that they throw a shadow from the pulpit on the congregation below them, — a shadow which they would have you think is cast by the argent wings of hovering angels, but whose chill suggests the transvolation of Lucifer with his pride-frosted host. Seldom is one of them so cordially imbued with pure Christianity as to be able to proclaim the anti-clerical spirit of Christ's teaching in tones so strong and clear as those that resound from one of their great colleagues, the earnest, truth-loving, high-hearted Robertson, who, in the opening of his profound and beautiful sermon on vicarious sacrifice, says : — "There were many causes which made the Saviour obnoxious to the Priests and Pharisees. If that teaching were once received, their reign was over : a teaching which abolished the pretensions of a priesthood, by making every man his own priest, to offer spiritual sacrifices to God ; which identifies Religion with Goodness, — making spiritual excellence, not ritual regularity, the righteousness which God accepts; which brought God within reach of the sinner and the fallen; which simplifies the whole matter, by making Religion a thing of the heart, and not of rabbinical learning or theology."

III.

Antwerp. — The Cathedral.

TO lure a stray sheep back into the fold, was an art which had no adepts in Antwerp. *Vexatio dat intellectum,* is a maxim of the Jesuits, and a wise one. The theologico-polemic intellect of the Antwerpians had not been shaken up for many a long year; it slept the sound sleep of priest-paralized generations. I doubt whether the whole city or province could have furnished a champion tolerably equipped for encounter with a heretic, even with a green one. They had been taught — and had learnt the lesson well — not to argue about religion; but to accept it trustfully from the priest. Open your mouth and shut your eyes, as we say to children. Pure religion can only come to men through the Church, is a kind of donation from the Church: this brazen blasphemy is a fundamental Romish assumption: and you are not to look a gift horse in the mouth. Nor was there any desire to. To those who are cradled in it the Catholic is a most easy, well-cushioned creed. In all countries, but especially in those that have been long priest-ridden, the number of people who are moved to think for themselves is small, and many of those so moved suppress the motion. The mass of Catholics, when cut off from intercourse with Protestants, not only *have* no doubts, but *know* of none. And this they are taught to regard as a blessed mental state! Even the clergy of Antwerp — probably not chosen for their Aristotelian capabilities — lived so mechanic a life intellectually, and one so unagitated theologically, that they could hardly have put forward a skilful argumentative litigant. Nay, had recourse been had to the neighboring See of Malines, it may be questioned whether the Archbishop himself would have been found ready with a dialectic apparatus that would have enabled him to cut a triumphant figure in such an enterprise, even supposing that his Grace would have condescended to lend a leg to catch a runaway.

My uncle, who had spent his early manhood in Protestant America, was nevertheless as much unfurnished as any for laying siege to a heretic. He did not like trouble. His own religion had never given him any; if that can be called his, which he avowedly left to the keeping of his confessor. In his cerebral battery the tube of veneration, and the coadjuvant tubes of hope and wonder, were of moderate size, and thus not capable of carrying a large or continuous charge. In the higher sensibilities he was not rich, and thence he had no sustained thoughtfulness for religious questions, the settlement of all which he delegated to priests. That, said he, was their business ; they were brought up to it. They had served the due apprenticeship at the art and mystery of furnishing garments to keep the soul comfortable. The priest was my uncle's spiritual tailor ; and he was not more exacting towards his spiritual clothes than towards his corporal, that they should be a close fit. I am confident that he and his confessor got on smoothly together. Most Catholics, who live on their incomes, I suspect, do. He knew how to make things " pleasant " between him and his Church. The Church always wants money, never has or can get enough of it. " Provide neither gold nor silver nor brass in your purses." My uncle, on account of bodily infirmities, bought of the Church (the sum paid was I think one hundred dollars annually) a dispensation to eat meat on fast days. His health would probably have been better had he abstained from meat on Mondays and Tuesdays as well as on Fridays and Saturdays. But he and his doctor thought otherwise ; and so he dealt in *indulgences* as buyer.

But for the religiously enervating atmosphere in which he had lived so long, and the insufflation of his zeal through feminine air-pipes, my uncle would not have taken my heresy much to heart. His was not a mind to meddle with other people's condition, mental or physical. He found enough to do to take care of himself. For others he had neither much condemnation nor much sympathy. He inclined to the doctrine of "Every man for himself, and God for us all,"—a doctrine which, could it become universally prevalent, would turn out to be equivalent to "Every man for himself, and the Devil take the hindmost;" and every man would be hindmost. Besides, he had been liberalized by travel. He had visited the best of Europe; had lived in America, where he had seen a Bishop (Bishop White of Philadelphia) surrounded by his wife and children,—a startling spectacle to a Catholic; had been to Mount Vernon and had talked with Washington.

And here let me report a remark made to him by Washington, a remark in its naked self insignificant, but clothed with importance when regarded as corroborative of the probity of nature, unfailingly exhibited by that exalted man, in small things as well as great. My uncle's attention being attracted to the sculptured marble mantelpiece before them in the drawing-room, Washington told him that it was a present from his friend, Marquis La Fayette, adding,—"They tell me it is a fine piece of work; but of that, you, sir, can judge much better than I; for I have no knowledge of the arts."

I continued to accompany my uncle to the

cathedral. The service recommended itself, especially to impatient youth, by its brevity. It lasted not more than half an hour, often less. Sermons we never heard. There were sermons occasionally, but except when some rare orator can be listened to, sermons in the Catholics churches of Europe are for the unreading multitude. In the Catholic Church sermons are altogether secondary. The Church does not encourage them. To prepare a sermon requires more or less of individual thought. The sermonizer falls back on his own resources. He must think; and the Church does not like to set any one to think. A thinking priest, who gives utterance to his thoughts, will set some of his auditors a-thinking, and thus is a crevice opened through which the Devil is sure to creep. No pulpit is a place for the widest mental range. I have heard of a Protestant clergyman who preached himself out of his own pulpit, the momentum imparted to his mind by the exercise of thought in writing sermons having wafted him up into a region more free and sunny than that where his pulpit was anchored.

On the vast floor of the cathedral we generally placed ourselves where we could take in a view of the *Descent from the Cross* of Rubens. The spiritual and corporeal grandeur of this magnificent work, the strength combined with grace in the figures and in the grouping of them, the strain without distortion in the efforts and limbs of the principal agents in lowering the body, the pathetic tenderness with which they handle the body, all of them proclaiming by look and posture and gesture how holy they regard it, the dignity and majesty stamped upon the compact group, the repose in the midst of action, the balanced splendor of the coloring, and, irradiating and giving to the whole its great power, the lofty life wherewith the whole and all the parts are instinct, as it were from within,—these rare and varied and combined excellences carry into the mind an impression so full and elevating and enduring, as to justify the judgment of many, that this is among pictures the masterpiece of the world.

The picture and the sublime architecture about it grew on me weekly. Not so the performances at the altar. It was indeed an imposing and profitable introduction to the Art of Europe, to become at the outset familiarized—if it can be said that one ever becomes familiar—with such vast creations. It might be thought that I would have associated them with the services. By no means. They were to me grand and elevating; they fed the growth of my mind; they wrought upon my imagination, much more than I was conscious of at the time. They remain ever fresh and inspiring. The services were from the first to me ineffective, empty; nay, petty and even frivolous.

The pious Catholic follows his accustomed ritual devoutly. In him the religious sentiment, habituated to this routine, repeats it fervently. The innate religious thirst in man slakes itself in part at certain stages of human development, in various kinds of rites and ceremonies, according to temperament and education, — rites and ceremonies which, being purely human, are in themselves barren, and are only then divine and fruitful when by those who follow them they are dilated by that which is divine in the heart. That the Catholic is content with that to which he is used, proves, what is equally proved by any other believers, that there is in man an inborn revering element; that man is a religious being; that is, he is a link, and a moving link, in the endless chain that stretches from the earth up through the Infinite towards the Eternal God; and that through this mighty privilege he has within him a holiness allied to the All-Holy. And this deep, exhaustless fund, this it is on which self-seeking hierarchies draw, and which they as trustees so grossly misuse. They would, and often do, make their followers believe, that what *they* give, that is, the forms and rituals and sacraments, are the main thing; not what God gives, that is, the inward need of communion with him, with the expansive, fortifying effects of its healthful, simple satisfaction. Whereas the God-given is the all in all; the man-contrived is comparatively pithless and powerless, deriving what potency it may have, and all its healing virtue, from the presence and power of the other. The way in which a man prays, or puts himself in communication with the all-enfolding Godhead, the means to which he betakes him to vivify, to intensify, the presence of the divine within him, these are no more than the casket which holds the jewels. Priesthoods — who are the makers and venders of the caskets — would persuade us that these are primary, and that without them we should have no jewels. Just leave your casket in their keeping, and they will polish and burnish it so that you would hardly know it; and you will find, that most of the jewels have been transferred from the inside of the casket to enrich its outside.

Look at the Vatican and the Quirinal, and the scarlet sumptuosities of Cardinal Eminences, at the multiform carnalities of prelates, at Episcopal palaces and vainglorious titles on the Continent and in England, and the fat livings and flattering temporalities and graceless enjoyments of so many priests, Protestant as well as Catholic. All these enjoyments are at the expense, not merely of the spirituality of the enjoyers, but of that of their ecclesiastical adherents. Nature is inviolable. You cannot feed her lungs through her ears. She demands like unto like. Full flesh-pots breed lean spirits. You cannot eat your cake and have it. The priest who is beset by longings for fame or place or power or luxury (and some lust for them all) has swallowed his spiritual cake, and has none to share with you or me. Spirituality and worldliness are not antagonistic merely, they are reciprocally internecive. Pomp and Christianity, self-seeking and devotion, priestly pretension and manly purity, are as incompatible as God and Mammon.

Worldly priests — and how many are they ? — undevout priests — and how many are they ? — are gamblers in souls. But as counters to score their own earthly gains do they hold the members of their flock. The richer therefore these are in worldly goods, the more acceptable. The deep, sacred aspirations of the soul they turn into breath to blow the trumpets of their fame. They fan the flame of the spirit, that it may warm their kitchens. The holiest fire of creation, to which all vestal-watched fires are ashes, to which the sparkle of stars is blackness, — this ye would handle to make your pots boil, to light up the ghastly glare of your palaces, to feed your selfish heats. Sacrilegious charlatans! profane buffoons! what report shall be yours in the accounting days of eternity?

A comforter, not a director, the priest should be; an aid, not a chief; a sympathizing helper, not an authoritative dispenser. His best and fruitfulest service were, to teach and help men to be each one his own priest. For the higher functions of associated life, and even for the lower, Nature provides agents specially endowed. The God-sent priest is known by his spirituality. Less clogged is his freedom by the weights of the world than that of other men; the play of his heart less obstructed by fleshly obesities. A transcendental cheer irradiates his earnestness, making trust in him a lively joy to all who seek him, as well as a solid reliance. Among his fellows he moves with a super-earthly springiness, as though his shoulders were armed with invisible wings, lent him by fraternal angels. His diploma is his unselfishness; his heavenward affinities are his ordination; his sympathies with his brother-men are his election to pastorship. He is entitled to be called a "divine," because in his thoughts and wishes there is more of divinity than in those of most men, and less proud and earthy are his desires. Like Chaucer's poor parson,—so transpicuously delineated in the Prologue to the "Canterbury Tales,"—his wealth of holy thought shows itself in his work. Like Chaucer's exquisite archetype, "He could in litel thing have suffisance;" and like him sets this high example, "That first he wrought and afterward he taught."

A great priest, F. W. Robertson,—from whom I have already quoted,—great by his spirituality and intellectuality and truthfulness, says, "God's power, God's life — wherever these exist, *there* there is a sacrament. What is the lesson then which we learn? Is it that God's life, and love, and grace are limited to certain materials, such as the Rock, the Bread, or the Wine? is it that we are doing an awful act only when we baptize? or is it not much rather, that all here is sacramental, that we live in a fearful and a divine world; that every simple meal, that every gushing stream, every rolling river, and every drifting cloud, is the symbol of God, and a sacrament to every *open* heart? And the power of recognizing and feeling this makes all the difference between the religious and the irreligious spirit."

Now it is just this life of man in God, this life of man with God, that priesthoods would cut and do cut in twain. They thrust themselves between man and God. Without them there can be no sacraments! Out of man's life and natural feeling they take the holiness and transfer it to themselves. They degrade man and belittle God in bemonstering themselves. Look at that sensual face, made up for the moment into sacerdotal solemnity for administering the Eucharist. See him the next day, flattering Dives at his table, while Madame Dives picks out for him the choice bits. "But this is an extreme case." No, it is not an extreme case. It is, in different degrees, not an uncommon case. "But towards priests we should be charitable as towards other men." Aye, let the man have full charity, but not his priestly pretensions. These touch the deepest heart of human interests. Here is a fellow-man who is a transparent self-seeker and sensualist, to whom the clerical profession is obviously a trade, not a vocation, and who pretends to be especially qualified and authorized to put you and me in relation with God, and who moreover denies to us the power fully to do so without his intermediation. An ecclesiastical mannikin, often a dullard, oftener a worldling, sometimes both, arrogates to himself superhuman powers, calls himself "divine," plays God's vicar among men. The Impostor! The most that even St. Paul, or Oberlin, or Robertson can do is to help me, through spiritual sympathy. A most grave task it is for one man to offer himself as an intermediary between a brother man and God. Think of the awfulness of the function. To perform it at all, what piety must be present in the interpreter, what a flooding of his whole being with religious influx; and to find himself in this condition, what habitual heavenward aspiration, what cultivated tenderness of brotherly sympathy!

But religion must manifest itself in forms, and these require a dedicated class of men. Religion, to prove itself genuine, actual, must manifest itself in *acts*. Forms may be and often are utterly hollow semblances; acts can be but solid realities.

It is easy for a rich man, or for a number of men, to build a church; it is easy to attend service in it regularly; it is easy to repeat prayers. These are forms. Do they imply acts? rather the reverse; for even in those who are not frivolous or hypocritical, and who go through them with devoutness, these forms impose on the imagination, making themselves pass for acts. Religion being an invisible essence, which only in life, in daily doings, can be visibly embodied, if we do not live it we have little of it. Live as knowing and inwardly feeling ourselves to be beings who are to live forever, beings who belong to the Infinite and the Eternal, whose incommensurable privilege it is to feel, if we will, the hourly presence, the overlooking paternity of God; and thus our daily bearing will be much purged of littleness and lowness, of animalism and disloyalty. Solemn, loud-voiced prayers and serious looks and superficial hymning help us not to this living. They rather hinder us, by diverting our esteem from the thing to the show, from the substance to the form, and by tending to substitute a sentimental devoutness for a practical religious devotedness and dutifulness. Not lip and knee worship, but heart and head worship is demanded of us by God, for the real, not the seeming, satisfaction of that which is implanted in us by Him, — an immortal religious sentiment, which vainly seeks to fulfil its deep self through reiteration of conned words and ceremonial formalities.

IV.

Antwerp. — The Museum.

WHEN the short service in the Cathedral was over, my uncle moved toward the door, crossing himself; and the moment we were out, the whole proceeding was entirely behind and away from us, and we walked on, talking of temporal matters with as little devotion in our thoughts as there is of heavenward gratitude in those of a dress-dinner company just after grace. This keen division between the heavenly and the earthly, as if they were separate and hostile territories, is a feature of universal Christendom. Between the mundane and the supermundane there is a gulf, — not a natural gulf, but one worn artificially in a natural plane by the habit of devoting certain stated days and hours to worship, — a habit the tendency of which is to sunder religion from life. Across this gulf there is no bridge to heaven, which to those only is open into whose every-day being the religious and heavenly mingles as an element of working hours. The man who has not made for himself some heaven on earth will find none beyond the tomb. He will have to set to work there to make one.

Sometimes, on the Sunday forenoon, we went directly from the Cathedral to the Museum. At first the crowded expanse of pictures, like a well-dressed throng to a stranger, looked promiscuous. But a few visits, under the guidance of my uncle, brought out to me their individualities; and soon I grew worthy enough of their company to recognize the good from the bad, and then, by further growth of vision, the best from the better, these from the good, and these again from the indifferent.

In almost every large collection there is found a roomy limbo of mediocrity, and especially in the public Museum of a provincial town, where there will hardly be wealth of canvas and variety enough to bear so full an elimination as an exacting criticism would enjoin. Moreover, the picture-loving and picture-coveting world is possessed by a distressful plethoric canvas-conservatism. Nobody likes to burn a picture. A painted surface, with heads and figures and clouds and trees and fields, and a gilt frame, has *per se*, quality aside, a kind of sacredness in people's eyes. A feeling is this honorable to humanity, pointing to a latent faculty to honor Art. Nevertheless, could the innate faculty be unfolded up to the lucidness of vision that would lead to the conflagration of two thirds of the painted canvas in Christendom, Art and Humanity would not be the losers.

Galleries, public and private, are mostly loaded with pictorial platitudes. Many pictures, like many of their beholders, (and a full collection represents humanity, its high and low and the whole intermediate semi-vacuum of the indifferent,) have more pretension than capacity, ambition pushing them to try to *seem* what they have not inward life to *be*. Mechanical manipulation is superabundant in these latter days. I suppose two thirds of the younger portion of those one meets in walking down a crowded thoroughfare could be taught to draw; and through the publicity and pecuniary profitableness of the avocations that require knowledge of drawing, a multitude of people are proficients with the pencil. The facility in its use, like that of the pen to make verse, becomes often fatal, tempting many into a province for which they have neither the spirituality nor the intellectuality.

Genuine poetry is a new creation, the rhythmical result of a fresh original energy, working outward from the unseen focuses of feeling, — a novel incarnation of a novel spiritual impulse; and painted pictures, to be good, should be poetical; that is, even in their lowest form they should exhibit a fresh aspect won from reality by the light thrown on it from a penetrative beauty-enlightened mind. To work well with pen or brush a man must have in him a something new which craves utterance. In his brain must be born a somewhat that the world has not yet seen. By this inward birth he must be in a measure dominated. He becomes, and it is his joy to become, the mere tool of his intuitions and conceptions. Does he do his work from love of the work, or from love of himself? This is a life question. Upon it depends whether work be alive or dead.

The test of a high painter is, that he be able to paint a piece of Paradise. Now, Paradise never was yet on earth except partially and approximately. It lies folded within the heart of man as the lily lies in its bulb during winter. The man of genial gift can by heat of imagination urge a glimpse of it into flower on the canvas; that is, through the visible creation at his disposal as means, through man, earth, and sky, and their infinite conditions, aspects, combinations, he can represent in their primitive purity feelings, sentiments, aspirations, — thus through his re-creative potency incarnating the invisible and spiritual.

Art is the projection of man out of himself, under poetic impulse and possession. Thence the forms into which he throws himself will aim to express the best there is in him; for the poetic impulse is ever an impulse upward. Pictures ought to be, and good pictures are, a reduplication of our better selves. They give the echo to the healthier, higher feelings, — an echo that sometimes comes from above the clouds, and draws us up towards the impenetrable into which it fades.

Gaze, when in that highest state of earthly human being, a religious, poetic mood, (and the gazing will feed, and sometimes create, the mood,) at a river, or a mountain, or the ocean, or a child, and you are lifted into ineffable admiration and wonder and awe at the uncompassable might of the Maker. Secondary and akin to this is the feeling on beholding a reproduction of these objects by the hand of man, — a creative reproduction. And in addition to, and quite independent of, the spiritual satisfaction enjoyed through the presentation of such elevating subjects, there is a high joy — enhancing the other — in the contemplation of the human power exhibited; a power born and fed by the divine there is in man. What might and beauty there must be in the mind that could move and guide a human hand to put on canvas that face of the boy Jesus in the Madonna di Santo Sisto at Dresden, or that other of the great Murillo in the National Gallery at London, or that central head of divine grandeur and grace in the *Last Supper* at Milan. Thus a part, and hardly a minor part, of the enjoyment, the exaltation, in surveying works of Art, is admiration of, and sympathy with, the life in the brain of man, that could so reproduce God's work.

But, for a full, lasting effect, a picture must be much more than imitative; mere copying of forms and colors is dead. The representation must be so electrical with mental fire that it shall kindle power in the mind of the beholder. To his image the artist must impart a flush of life; the arteries must throb as they do in the leg of the Borghese Gladiator in the Louvre. For vivid, enduring embodiments the artist's brain must be so conceptive as to hold in it with fiery force the object of his perception or his imagination; and then so potent-plastic as to throw it forth again transfused with a poetic light. He must so love the object that he sees or imagines, as to seize it with a parental fulness and definitiveness, and then lay it upon the canvas with so light and sure a hand that it shall glow for ages with the warmth of his own heart.

A true painter, a born painter, is a man who, had he been born without fingers, would have forced his toes into the service of his teeming, formative brain; and had he been born blind, would have dictated to an expert amanuensis the beautiful pictures that crowd upon his inward vision, importuning him for deliverance. By this extravagence I wish to emphasize the preëminence of the spiritual and poetical over the material and mechanical.

My uncle was a connoisseur. He had fed on pictures since his childhood; and his mind being in its texture and temperament sufficiently æsthetic to assimilate such food, he enjoyed an appreciation of Art above that of the mere gentlemanly amateur. In recognition hereof he had been chosen by his native city one of its commissioners, sent to Paris in 1815 to reclaim from the Louvre Antwerp's share of the Art-treasures which the semi-barbarous hand of the Imperial spoiler had sequestered from the public galleries of the conquered continent, to adorn and spiritualize his gross ephemeral power.

My mother's father had a collection which was probably not surpassed in its day by any private one (out of Italy and England and Vienna) in Europe. It embraced the *Chapeau de Paille* of Rubens, and the *Le Roy* and his wife of Vandyke. At his death in 1821 the whole collection was sold at public sale in Antwerp. The *Chapeau de Paille* was bought for three thousand pounds by an English picture-dealer, who, after exhibiting it profitably for some time in London, sold it to Sir Robert Peel for, I think, five thousand. I presume that were it now put up at auction in London it would bring ten thousand pounds. The two full-length portraits of *Le Roy* and his wife were bought by my uncle, who would not see them sacrificed. I was present when, in 1823, he resold them to the Prince of Orange. They were esteemed two of the finest Vandykes extant, and the Prince had been for some time negotiating to get them. But his Royal Highness, a lavish spender, was generally "hard up," and being accounted rather bad pay, my uncle refused to let him have them except for cash in hand. At last the Prince, having agreed to this condition, fixed a day when he would come to close the bargain.

My uncle, tall, straight, thin, but not wanting in breadth (what the French call *un gros maigre*) had the high-bred manners of the old *régime*, simplified by travel and sojourn in republican America. He received the Prince with the mixture of ease and deference and kindness which became a subject on such an occasion toward the throne's heir. The Prince was a *blond*, with florid complexion, of light build, and sprightly, amiable countenance, about five feet seven or eight inches in height. After gazing in undisguised admiration at the tall, stately, graceful canvas-figures, he turned to the owner and asked his price. My uncle, with a little heightened cordiality and deference in his manner, as if to efface the offence of questioning the solvability of his sovereign's first-born, — handed him a slip of paper on which were written, he told him, the final terms, — five thousand dollars, I think, for the two. The Prince cast his eye on the paper, put it into his pocket, bowed, and retired. In a few days the cash came, and these masterpieces were borne off to Brussels.

My uncle's excuse for selling them to the Prince of Orange was, that thereby they would be preserved to Belgium, a calculation wherein he wofully misreckoned; for when, only a few years later, in 1831, the family of Orange was driven (by aid of the French) out of Belgium, the Prince carried his collection of pictures with him to the Hague; and there, at his death in 1849, they—being his private property—were sold to pay his debts. For *Le Roy* and wife there was lively competition, the agent of the Louvre running them up to seventy-five thousand francs (about fifteen thousand dollars) for which sum they were bought by the Marquis of Hertford.

When towards the end of the last century my grandfather emigrated, designing to make America his home, he brought his pictures with him; and when in 1805 he was obliged to return to Belgium, they were left behind for greater security, having been carefully packed by his order, ready to be shipped at any moment. But there being uninterrupted war in Europe, they remained for ten years boxed up on the lower floor of a wing of my father's house, whence in case of fire they could have been easily removed. In 1816, my grandfather sent for them. They were now all taken out of the cases to be repacked; and my father and mother, feeling that it would almost be a public wrong that such a collection of pictures—the like of which had never been in America — should pass out of the country entirely unenjoyed, gave public notice that they could be seen for two or three weeks. Many persons came out from Washington, and from the neighborhood, to our house near Bladensburg, and several all the way from Philadelphia.

One box had been opened for a few days, several years before, for the eminent American portrait-painter, Gilbert Stuart, on the occasion of his spending a fortnight at my father's to paint the portraits of him and my mother.

A few weeks after my arrival at Antwerp, we moved into town. Besides the academic walks through the Museum, I now had lessons at home in architecture from a professor of that art. I should rather say, I had lessons in the mechanism of the Greek columnar styles. I became acquainted with the external characteristics of the three orders. I learned the shapes and names of dentils and modillions and mouldings, and all about the entablature and its division into architrave, frieze and cornice. But of the life and growth of these members and constituents, and of the column itself, and how it came to be, I learned nothing. The *Laws* which govern buildings in all their purposes and proportions — how use and beauty may be harmonized, how the idea controls the work, and how only idea can give life to work — of all this there was no word; nor of the relation between the architecture of a people and its mind,—its wants and its aspirations.

Now not only the best way, but the only good way, to teach even the very young, is through principles. Children are eager for the why and the wherefore; and the boy who breaks his drum to discover the cause of its sound, is in the widest sense representative. Much earlier than most people are aware, youthful minds not only grasp principles, but take in statements that involve large ideas, and carry the thoughts high and far. The whole they will of course not take in, but enough to be a germ, and a germ that will instinctively feed itself by clasping roots round many particulars. Put a good principle into the mind, and upon it you can securely hang scores of facts, and series of facts, which without this hold will soon drop out or be effaced.

My Professor was, physiognomically, one of those exceptional men whom one occasionally meets, and more often, perhaps, in continental cities than elsewhere,—men who in the mingling together of races and families seem to have been underkneaded, overlooked on the edge of the tray, and come out of the oven marked with singularity. He had much of an Indian's complexion and face, with straight, black, unelectrified hair and pyramidal head, his forehead being much broader at the base across the eyes than where it curved into the coronal region, — a shape which excludes, in the man or race in whom it is found, all poetic susceptibility and artistic liveliness. Luckily for him, his architectural ambitions did not outsparkle those of his neighbors. Antwerp was for the time architecturally finished; there was no room there then for creation or invention. To keep the old in repair, or at most to reproduce it, is the limit of a builder's function in a stagnant city, whose glories are in memory rather than in hope.

Had my uncle and the professor taken me to the Cathedral; led me down into the vaults; pointed out the deep broad foundations; then built up before my eyes the vast structure, stage by stage, exhibiting to me the high mechanical knowledge displayed in the superposition of such upstretching masses crowned by the gigantic roof; then aroused and enlightened my poetic sensibilities by making me a witness to the marriage of use to grandeur and beauty, — the solid walls, through the mystic power of poetic art, standing there before me without heaviness, the lofty, light, upspringing colonnades without weakness, — just hinting at the conditions of this union; then educated my perception to the purpose and grace of the manifold details; and then, finally, presented to my now enlarged perception, the whole, inside and out, in all its aërial vastness, its roomy magnificence;—had this been done, I should, even in a short series of lessons, have taken in much of the very essence of architecture. The great building, and with it all building, would have mingled itself in nervous movement, in imposing power, with my higher faculties. I should have carried away vital knowledge, which would have been a light in my mind forever. But for this kind of teaching the teachers are yet few, and from the primary school to the æsthetic academy, routine as method, and memory as means, are more suitable to the capacities of instructors than are lively, confident appeals to the reason and the nobler sensibilities.

For such impressive, attractive initiation, my uncle was not disposed or qualified, for he was an accomplished dilettante, not an earnest student of art.

Unless men handle actively the thoughts and institutions which they inherit as a golden bond of power, adding by strenuous invention fresh links to give themselves a purchase on the present and future, the past becomes a tightening halter that strangles their freedom. My professor wore his part of the chain quiescently, passively, unconsciously; nor was my uncle himself—with far higher capabilities — at all aware to what degree he was benumbed by the exanimate air of custom.

The autumn had worn away; winter had come; and I was still at Antwerp. The domestication under his childless roof of a fresh full-grown nephew from the new world was an event in the quiet, comparatively vacant, life of my uncle. People who live in industrial inaction on their incomes, and who lack mental force or impulsiveness to create immaterial interests, moral, intellectual, or æsthetic, have to do daily battle with Time; for Time will kill them if they cannot kill him. To maintain the fight they are obliged — humiliating obligation — to make the prosaic means of life its end; so that meals, — purposely prolonged, — and dressing, and distant supervision of pecuniary interests, and minor social duties, and exercise, become their occupations, wherewith by aid of the amusements of visiting, passive reading, small talk, games, cards, tobacco, they fill the vacuum left by sleep. My uncle used tobacco in no form; and cards I never saw in his house.

The recurrent routine of my uncle's day was suddenly broken and enlivened by my arrival. I became at once an object to his intellect and his affections. My heresy did not, as I have intimated, much disturb him individually; for he was a man of good understanding, and although not of large power of sympathy, had lived long enough in amicable contact with persons of variant religious convictions not to feel by habit the absurd unhumanity of that shallow self-righteousness which feeds a spurious piety with the poisoned drippings of arrogance, and, born of conceit and nourished by priestcraft (Protestant as well as Catholic) for its own perverted ends, makes a fallible, and mostly an ignorant and limited individual, ascribe infallibility to his religious conceptions, and pass on all dissentients a fire-freighted anathema.

But amidst the members of an ancient Catholic society, the bricks of whose fabric were moulded centuries ago, and the mortar of their present cohesion compounded of traditions and conventionalities, a young, American, republican Protestant, though neither froward nor demonstrative, was as unfitting as a Gothic spire on an Ionic temple, as intrusive almost as an eel among crabs. The protestantism, the chief source of incongruity, might possibly be wiped out, and with a view to such an end my uncle would have liked to change my route of travel on leaving Antwerp, making it lead to Paris instead of Goettingen. On his hinting this to me, I objected that my father's wish was that I should go to Goettingen. Had the change found favor with myself, he would, I am sure, have written at once to my father recommending it.

A curious episode it was in my opening life, those three months spent in Antwerp with my uncle and aunt; and his image and hers come to me across the crowded current of forty years with kindly smiling features, in colors all harmonized by the cheerful light cast by the trustful transfiguring eyes of youth.

V.

From Antwerp to Goettingen.

ON the fourth of January, 1824, I set out for Brussels with my uncle, who devoted two days to showing me the palaces and pictures of the capital. At Laeken, the summer palace of the King, — where I saw an orangery three hundred years old, — the bed-chamber of the Queen gave occasion in my journal to the following scrap of reasoning, which, if not exhaustive of the subject treated, nor allured into philosophic or historic channels, shows at least that the faculties of the incipient traveller were disposed to try themselves on solutions. — "Curtains of the bed beautiful: coverlet of a light blue, velvet and gold, worked by the Empress Josephine: a large J. in gold in the middle of it. Singular that it should be used. One of two reasons must be allowed: either it is from regard to the first owner, or else because it is thought not worth while to purchase a new one where one so rich may be had for nothing."

We went into a bookstore to buy a "Traveller's Guide." The title of a volume attracted me, and the table of contents strengthening the attraction, I bought the book, — a French volume of Essays, just published. The subjects were those large warm ones that have an unfading fascination, even when in maturer years the studious reader has discovered that sounding titles are mostly promises to the eye that are broken to the hope. Themes there are that give such assurances to the deathless yearnings of the human heart for a better life, that their freshness cannot be worn off by endless repetition through the barren pens of the unimaginative and the unspiritual.

My uncle could not conceal his vexation. To buy a printed pig in a poke was to him the most senseless kind of improvidence. It might be worse than throwing away five francs; it was probably the planting of fallaceous seed that would come up weeds. My uncle was not an habitual reader of books, new or old. He had a small collection shelved, hidden I might say, in a large closet, picked up mostly in foreign lands, and partially read. But they were not active members of his household; they were not allowed to do even as much service as mirrors. To him they were little better than the lumber in his garret.

In those days there was in Antwerp but one bookstore, and that a meagre one; and in later years, on my revisits, the book-business was not much livelier. Reading is discouraged by the Romish priesthood. The body that puts a ban upon *the Book* is but logical in discountenancing all books. A present convocation of Rome's staunchest Bishops would not take it as a libel, but as a tribute, to be charged with harboring the wish that printing had not been and could never be invented. A class of men who believe that it would be safer for humanity that *they* should do all the thinking, would like to do all the reading. Hence in countries under full Catholic sway there are no public yearly-growing accumulations of miscellaneous books, and private libraries are rare. I doubt whether in Antwerp there was a single citizen who had books enough to be called a library. For every volume printed or circulated in Austria there are probably twenty in Prussia.

My uncle once related to me, that a friend of his had in early manhood indulged an omnivorous appetite for heretical and "infidel" reading. My aunt, who was by, assisted him in the relation with such an alarmed sensibility, that, with aid of some other hints, I was entitled to believe, that the edaceous foul-feeder was a near relative of hers. The moral (and had there not been this moral to the story I surely had never heard of it) was, that finding his faith thereby weakened, and his religious impressions confused, he, one blessed day, renounced his evil pages forever, and relapsed into mental quiescence, and the comforts of the confessional.

He was one of those half-educated men, not capable indeed of a whole education, — a numerous class, — whose moral manhood falls short of self-sufficiency, and who, though coiled about in youth by the cramping bandages of dogma and creed, and taught to mistrust the man within them, and to trust a man outside of themselves, have yet in stouter years the wish to break into the fruitful freedom of individual thought; but, partly from spiritual weakness, and partly for personal ease, after an effort or two, redeliver themselves into bondage, pusillanimously playing into the hands of spiritual despots.

But thanks to a long line of moral heroes, men with Christ-like spirit, and intellects vividly piercing, — the providential educators and foremen of humanity, — priesthoods and dogmas have lost the worst of their power, and are fast losing their sanctity, which, factitious in them, is restored to where alone on earth it is genuine, — to the *soul of man.* Not to learn from priests did the boy Jesus go into the temple, but to dispute with and confound them. And so long as priests shall exist, will they need to be disputed with and confounded. The foremost and broadest assertor of the grandeur and self-sufficiency of the soul is He whose great doctrines were preached in God's roofless temple, with fields and mountains for altars, and the toiling multitude for listeners. To think what a figure He would cut in a carpeted city church, with its cushioned exclusive pews, amid the millinery and haberdashery, and the rustling, restless vanity of a modern congregation; or beside the embroidered priest, with his stale formularies and his pagan incense, — He, the practical protester against formalities and ostentations, who never did act or spoke word to put a brother man under spiritual bondage.

The returned fugitive of my uncle was like a traveller who, getting enveloped in mist on ascending a mountain, quickly retraces his steps in alarm. Had he pushed upward he would soon have attained to magnificent prospects bathed in light, leaving behind him the mist, which moreover was thickened by his fears and his ignorance.

Who doubts that it were better for any man, even when no longer young, not to consort with men habitually immoral or vicious. But free choice of companionship can be denied to none except through tyrannous, destructive assault upon the personality. The danger of such assault to the spiritual life of mankind were as a thousand to one to the dangers flowing from its freedom. The companions of a man's solitude — his books not less than his thoughts — claim, for the same paramount reason, exemption from control or interference. The Romish Church has always aimed, not to control merely, but to crush man's spiritual freedom, and this usurped privilege to proscribe books is but one of its means of defiling the deepest of human sanctities. Read its list of condemned books, the "Index Prohibitorum Librorum," to learn the mingled folly and arrogance of this proscription.

Her high priests would press their armed fingers on the inmost centres of mental power to paralyze the very sources of thought and moral life, so ravenous is their greed of rule, so insidiously remorseless their means. Books are the life and the evidence of life in man's upper world — his world of meditation. They are at once the reservoirs and the conductors that gather, preserve, and transmit, from generation to generation, the finer spirit of humanity. Books are the very hour-hands of Time, his measurers and sanctifiers. Without them he is a barbarian and childish idler, with neither skill nor will to plant mile-stones along his track, whereby men shall hereafter both learn of his being and be helped on their way. Without them Time leaves behind him a waste so unfurrowed and unemphasized, that a people, among whom he is thus uncreative, has no history, and so poor a life —

> That dim oblivion weighs upon the breath
> Of its Lethean air.

On the third day I took leave of my uncle, and mounted into a *diligence* to resume my so long-interrupted journey to renowned Goettingen. We started at seven, to breakfast between ten and eleven, twenty miles distant, at Louvain, famed for its Gothic *Hotel de Ville*, in ancient times for its University, and in modern for its beer. My seat was in the central compartment of the huge *diligence*. The stage-coach in America or England was a more sociable vehicle than the railroad car; and the continental *diligence* was more sociable than the coach. Three of my four fellow passengers were a father and mother, with a grown-up daughter, from Lille in France, just over the Belgian border, going to see their sons, students in the University of Liege. They were samples of the *bourgeoisie* of France and Belgium, superior samples, being kindly and comely and prosperous and worthily aspiring — as the cause of their journey proved — and of a moral tone that sharpened their parental instincts against Paris as a finishing school for youth.

They belonged to that class in Europe who, in dedicating themselves to garnering the material harvests of human labor, become in their minds more materialized, not only than the better-educated classes above them, but than the crowd of drudging hand-workers below them, but who, if somewhat debased by the habits of traffic, have often shown politically a brave steadfastness and a manly appreciation of freedom that have told momentously upon the history and advancement of Europe. From drawing the fat of the land to their purses and persons, men of this condition are mostly earthy and material in their wants and ambitions, and thence have furnished but a small proportion of the spiritual and intellectual benefactors of mankind. From this unctuous class have not sprung the mental leaders — Paul and Socrates and Galileo and Dante and Abelard and Savonarola and Luther and Cervantes and Wycliffe and Shakespeare and Bacon and Descartes and Spinoza and Pascal and Kant and Milton and Newton and Burns and Gall and Fenelon and Swedenborg and Franklin and Wordsworth and Coleridge — men whose thoughts are Heaven's dowry to man, and their doings and memories his most precious heir-looms.

Goethe is the only exception I can recall of a man of high mental endowment and enduring power who issued directly from the trading class. And he is only a partial exception; for, while his paternal grandfather was a prosperous publican, the keeper of one of the great inns of Frankfort, his maternal was a distinguished legist and the descendant of a line of juridical celebrities; and Goethe's father not only did not succeed his sire as chief of the *Weidenhof Hotel*, but studied at the University of Leipzig, and took the degree of Doctor of Laws at that of Giessen; and after having further added to his intellectual stores by travel in Germany and Italy, devoted his mature years to study and music and drawing, thus planting his life, through spontaneous motion, in a soil where was to be reaped a harvest richer than ducats; and, by making himself a cultivated accomplished gentleman, became fit to be a serviceable assistant and instructor to his brilliant many-sided son.

We got to Liege for early bed-time. It was a long day's pull, seventy miles in fourteen hours. At breakfast the next morning appeared the sons, three of them, well-grown sprightly young men, who looked as though they were undergoing promotion out of the dense burgher medium into the rarer freer one of scholarship and disinterested thought. Unincumbered with adipose deposit, they gave no signs of future rotundity, while the daughter, pretty and full-faced, was palpably predestined to assume the prodigal plumpness of mamma.

Before breakfast I walked out to look at the University building, recently erected, the Church of St. Paul, and the arched bridge over the Meuse. My journal records, that the church was "not remarkable," and that the University was "a handsome building with a front of eight pillars of the Ionic order." — So I was endeavoring to profit by the late lessons in architecture.

Starting again eastward at ten, I had the

diligence and the cold all to myself to Aix-la-Chapelle. As we did not arrive till after dark, the bones of Charlemagne had to go unseen. The next morning at seven I pursued my journey toward the Rhine, eating a fast-day dinner — it being Friday and the population Catholic. The innkeeper, mistaking me for an Englishman, tried to extort five francs from me for his fleshless meal; I made him take three. The good macadamized road and rich country helped to lighten the hours, which my fellow-passengers rather incumbered, they being so heavy a set that I was better off the day before alone in the cold.

I know not (probably dinner was waiting for us at the inn) why on reaching Cologne I did not go down at once to the Rhine, to see it while there was yet daylight, for we dismounted from the *diligence* at the *Cour Impériale* at three. But it was dark when I went out with a guide, and through narrow, unpeopled, unlighted streets, came in a few minutes upon the famous river, whose historic presence I was aware of more through the ears than the eyes, as his swollen winter-flood went hurrying by to seek its first repose in the infinitude of the ocean, like a lusty turbid human life speeding restlessly onward in the dark towards the grave. Since 1824 Cologne has been awakened to something of its ancient animation by the steam-whistle; but then, along the edge of the rushing river it lay within its mediæval walls and towers, impoverished, squalid, stagnant — a gray crumbling skeleton of its former populous self.

A crow, wishing to pass from Cologne to Goettingen, would pitch his flight toward a point some degrees north of east, crossing the Rhine to bid it adieu. Straight lines, drawn to connect Cologne, Frankfort, and Goettingen, would make a pretty good right-angled isosceles triangle, with the right angle at Frankfort, and consequently the hypothenuse stretching from Cologne to Goettingen. An impatient courier, therefore, bound from Cologne to Goettingen, would endeavor to keep as faithfully under the crow's wings as the circuities of the post-road would permit. But Westphalia, lacking both cities and scenery, is to the traveller unfruitful, dull, monotonous; whereas the roundabout route through Frankfort, besides leading him along the most picturesque highway in Europe, has its stations marked by cities orient with historical or present attraction. Nevertheless, had there not been a grosser reason why I should take the longer route I should probably have taken the shorter. But between Antwerp and a small, distant, interior, uncommercial German town like Goettingen, there were no means of direct "credit" relations; and so Antwerp had to have recourse to Frankfort to establish, between the strong box of a banker and the student's pocket, that golden line of communication which is as indispensable to his success at the University as is the lecture-room or library.

At eight in the morning of the tenth of January 1824, I found myself booked for Coblenz in the public coach, which had now changed its fitting French name of *diligence* for the unfitting German one of *eilwagen* (haste carriage), a name the giving of which to a vehicle that achieved barely five miles an hour, can only be honestly accounted for by supposing it to have supplanted some old-time predecessor that compassed but three. We were now so far inland that none of my fellow-passengers had probably ever stood on the wharf of a larger sea-port, for I was the first American they had seen; and the surprise was ejaculative that I was white, and increased to wonder when they learnt that I had made the passage from America to Europe in only twenty days. At six we reached the *Hotel de Trèves* in Coblenz, and the theatre being next door to the hotel, I went into it.

It may seem an extravagant comparison, but, sitting in front of the stage, my sensation was like what might have been that of a Roman gladiator who should have looked into the dens and cages whence glared upon him the fiery eyes of the tigers and panthers he was about to encounter in the arena. As the words — so alive to my ears and so dead to my understanding — were hurled from the actors, the task I was about to buckle to came before me as a terror. Could I ever extract thought out of this senseless stridor! My ears were closed to every thing save a cacophany. The open-eared enjoyment of my neighbors was almost insulting. Despair grew darker as I listened, and my loneliness became so oppressive, sitting there the sole unparticipant auditor, that after a short endurance of aggravated humiliation, I went back to the hotel to seek some one who would not agonize my ears, but delight them with French or English syllables, and thus give me assurance that I was not utterly alone.

The coach for Mayence travelling all night, and there being no public conveyance by day, I engaged a post-chaise, and the next morning set out at eight. The day was cloudy and cold, yet I enjoyed the lonely drive up the smooth Rhine road through Boppart and St. Goar and Bingen. The Sunday stillness deepened the gray solemnity of winter, whose sunless atmosphere was congenial to the sombre, silent, hill-crowning ruins — grave mysterious companions to the traveller, one or more being always in sight, thus seeming to pass him on hospitably from stage to stage through their magnificent domain, lording it over the historical landscape like reserved, princely patricians. As I sat in a corner of the open post-chaise, I had, in the postilion and his horses, other and closer company, and the livelier, that the biting air made them trot to their quickest time, which was seven or eight miles an hour.

In my diary there is here an entry for which I cannot but take some shame to myself. At Ingelheim, between Bingen and Mayence, the last station for changing horses, "the innkeeper requested that a passenger might go with me to Mayence. I refused." — No reason is given for the refusal. I recollect the fact of the request, but nothing more. Whether, getting sight of the proposed companion, I liked not his look, or that the request of the innkeeper was not made with any vouching earnestness, or that there was a something in his manner which awakened suspicion, I cannot fully recall. There should have been some cause out of myself; for otherwise the refusal of what had probably been a most opportune service to the asker, and not even an inconvenience to the grantor, shows a disobliging humor not creditable to my humanity. At all events, the refusal standing naked and unaccounted for, I hereby reprove the young traveller, and thereby premonish all others of the same age.

Will the reader bear two or three days of the diary verbatim?

"*January* 12*th*, 1824; *Monday.* Crossed the Rhine in a boat; current strong and much ice —

bridge of boats removed during winter — mills in the middle of the river, turned by the force of the current. Started from Cassel, opposite Mayence, for Frankfort, in the cabriolet of diligence — weather gloomy and cold. Arrived at half-past two at Frankfort, and lodged at the *Hotel d'Angleterre;* good inn. Dressed, dined, and took a *domestique de place* to conduct me to Mr. E. Mueller — left the letter, which Mr. A. Cogels gave me at Antwerp, my card and address. Went to the opera at six. German music good; execution of orchestra admirable. Returned at nine and to bed.

"*January* 13*th*, *Tuesday.* Up at nine — breakfasted. Took a *domestique de place* and went to the Town-House — saw the famous *Bulle d'Or.* Inscription as follows; on one side, *Roma caput mundi*, *Regit orbis frœna rotundi.* On the other side, *Carolus Quartus*, *divina favente clementia*, *Romanorum Emperator semper Augustus*, *et Bohemiæ rex.* — Visited the Catholic Cathedral, ill-looking and dirty. Walked to the bridge; to the Library, just put up — Corinthian order with six pillars, not very remarkable — returned to hotel. Dined at the *table d'hote;* good dinner; took half a bottle of Burgundy — very good. Smoked a Spanish cigar. Made acquaintance of a Mr. Tuck — lively youth. Disappointed at not seeing or hearing from Mr. Mueller. Mr. Lippert, the landlord of the inn, took me to the reading-room under the Cassino. Took supper at eight, and went to bed at half-past nine.

"*January 14th, Wednesday.* Breakfasted at nine. Walked out to see pictures — one very fine of Teniers and one Italian. Went to see Mr. Mueller in his *comptoir* — presented me with a card of admission to the Cassino. Dined at one at *table d'hote;* sat next to an Englishman, Mr. Maude, on his way home from walking over Switzerland. Went to Cassino. Supper, and to bed at nine. Ennui."

From this last word I take a hint and close the diary.

The *Golden Bull*, whose inscription I so tenderly copied, had long had a corner in my memory, having been carefully placed there about the year 1818 by Mr. Constant, the capable principal of Mt. Airy Seminary, Germantown, Pennsylvania, who prided himself on his method of teaching history, which was, to stamp upon the learner's brain dates and prominent men and epochs by means of charts arranged in vertical columns of chronologically sequent events, so that, each important nation having a separate column, the synchronous events in all were on a horizontal level — a plan devised by a Frenchman, Le Sage or Lavoisne, several copies of whose large historical atlas Mr. C. had in French. This atlas was afterward translated and republished in America.

To hold in my very hand this compact piece of European history, there was an actualization of the boy's lesson beyond the dreams of the school-room. It sounds like a paradox, but the actualities of life as much exceed the dreams of boyhood as a sword of steel does in efficacy, and in brilliancy too, a sword of tin. Young dreams and hopes are illogical, vapory, amorphous, and what they essay to foreshow has the magnification, and therefore the falsity often, of forms seen through a mist. Bubbles they are that float off from the simmering caldron of crude desires. They denote toward which quarter the currents of a life would tend; but shattered by the gales and tempests of manhood, all trace of them on the brain is obliterated by the melting or scalding heats of after joys and sorrows. Different as blossom from seed are they from the ideals of mature years, which, growing out of a deep soil, are watered by the daily dews of a warm experience, and are purified by the incessant breath of mounting imaginations. But like them they serve to keep the heart buoyant and confident.

The *Golden Bull*, aside from its attractiveness to me through school-day associations, is a notable historical document, being a kind of German *Magna Charta*. It was an Imperial proclamation or decree, whose chief purpose was to define and consolidate the rights of the Prince-Electors.

As an acknowledgment or fortification of the rights of other classes or of the masses, it was of no account. A German historian (Luden) describes it as an instrument "which established more firmly the Electors of the Empire. The Empire, however, which rested on these pillars was, like the blue vault of heaven, nowhere to be laid hold of. The Emperor was enthroned in a vacuum, and the pillars were the only reality."

Both Empire and Electors have been swept away by the floods whose fountain was the French Revolution; and Frankfort, where sits the substitute for the Empire — the Diet of the unknit German Confederation — has, from that source, as little of the privileges and characteristics of a genuine Capital as it had when the Emperors were crowned within its walls. It is still but the Capital of a vacuum.

To the mind, resting on the history of a people, its being is embodied in the great men it has thrown up, their thoughts and their deeds. They give the history. Their birthplaces and their tombs are the shrines of the traveller. A great nation's past is a long variegated vista, aglow with coruscations from sages and warriors and statesmen and poets. Alfred and Chaucer and the Black Prince and Wycliffe and the Bacons and Sir Thomas More and Elizabeth and Raleigh and Shakespeare and Cromwell and Milton and Newton and Nelson and Wellington and Wordsworth represent England. They are her chartered ambassadors, accredited as well to our judgment as to our imagination.

It is significant that on Germany's roll of power there is a preponderance of men of thought over men of action. In kings and emperors she is weak. Few military or civic leaders has she whose deeds can match the words of her Luthers and Kants and Keplers and Leibnitzes and Lessings and Goethes and Schillers and Galls and Hegels and Richters and Humboldts. Between Herrman and Frederick of Prussia lies a tract of seventeen centuries, desert for long reaches in active mastership. Up through the great century of the Reformation Frederick the Wise, of Saxony, and Charles V. rear themselves high enough to be seen by distant ages; and following them and the offspring of that deep movement for mental emancipation, shine out Bernard of Weimar and Frederick William, "the Great Elector," of Brandenburg.

Of the transcendent glory of Frankfort among German cities I then had hardly a faint apprehension; for I had not happened to have read — what alone of Goethe was in that day accessible to foreigners — "The Sorrows of Werter," the English translation of which having been made from a loose French one, would stand to the original as would the refuse from the reeky tub of a sluttish washerwoman, stinted in water, to the clear abundant current of a bubbling spring. Goethe was remote and nebulous. The sweet, sightly, succulent ears of his wisdom lay buried to me in the multiplex husks of German verbs, adjectives, nouns, adverbs. Even when, on leaving Germany, I brought away a key to all the riches of a great language, its deepest treasure could only be partially valued; for it is a profound virtue of this poet-sage that his meanings reveal themselves but dimly to the young and the uncultivated. His are pages to delight and enlarge seasoned chastened minds; and in our later years the quiet emanations from his genius still fire in us trains that but for them would have lain latent forever, arousing and refreshing us through commixture of their life with ours, like the rays of an afternoon sun striking upon a line of pictures, that answer their welcome streak with a mellow glow and new exhibitions of character.

From his secluded Olympian height in Weimar Goethe occasionally descended into the busy frequented flats of his native city. His fellow-townsmen made much of him; for it would be difficult to find a German town, however prosaic its procedures, that would not recognize, even if it could not fully prize, intellectual or æsthetic eminence. Goethe, whose mother lived to a ripe old age in Frankfort, and who, in his many-sidedness and clear-sightedness, knew the value of all kinds of activities, enjoyed, no doubt, after a fashion, these visits. In one of his letters to Schiller he draws an illustration from his townsmen which contains a quiet irony on all trading competition. Schiller had written that Herder, in a letter to him, had intimated that he, Schiller, had plagiarized his *Diver* from one Nicholas Pesce. Goethe, writing from Frankfort in August 1797, thus refers to this part of Schiller's letter: — "I heartily pity the old man on the Topfberg, that he is doomed, through God knows what strange temper, to obstruct the path of himself and others on his own ground. There I like a thousand times better the Frankfort bankers, merchants, brokers, traders, Jews, gamblers, and jobbers, who at any rate bring somewhat to pass for themselves, although they trip up other people's heels."

Notwithstanding the *ennui* recorded at the end of my third day at Frankfort, I tarried there through the week "seeing sights," driving into the country, and going to the opera. On Monday noon, the nineteenth, with a letter of credit on Goettingen and a hundred silver florins in my pocket, I took passage in the public coach, which travelling day and night, with stops for meals, reached Cassel on Wednesday morning. It was a dreary depressive journey, made so in part by my companions, male and female, not one of whom could speak a word of English, and two or three only a little Teutonic French. They seemed to be mostly second and third class traders, people limited and ignorant and gross, the edges of whose selfishness had not been smoothed by lively attrition, much less aerated by contact with the upper strata of intellectual culture. Glad was I to stretch my legs and lungs in Cassel, whence in the afternoon, by the same conveyance, I started for Goettingen.

VI.

Goettingen.[1]

ABOUT nine o'clock on the evening of Wednesday, January twenty-first, 1824, the *Eilwagen* came to a grateful halt. I was at the end of a wearisome journey. The subaltern at the gate, having in a few moments assured himself that we were not a perfidious Grecian horse, but his honest old accquaintance, the slow coach, from Cassel, bade our patient conductor "Forwards;" and I entered the town of Goettingen.

An American youth, dropped down on a winter night into a German University, in the heart of strange Germany, deaf and dumb as to the speech around him, not within hundreds of miles of a being who knew his name or nature, or cared whether the next night he slept in his bed or his coffin: there was an hour for wailing homesickness. But youth is at once brave and plastic, manfully breasting adversities, and, at the same time, shaping itself fluently — body and mind — to immediate pressures; and finding ever a zest

1 This chapter on Goettingen, and the eighth, on Weimar, were published in 1856 in *Putnam's Magazine*.

in new conditions, those even that are the least sunny. I was not in redundant spirits, but yet I went thankfully to bed in the Crown Inn, and slept the sleep of healthy youth.

In the morning, loneliness grasped me more stringently, as though the light of day illuminated my isolation, and made it painfully sensible. But in my pocket I had, along with a dinner-vouching letter of credit, other less carnal epistles, which were sure to be honored as drafts on hospitality. These I made haste to deliver in the forenoon. An hour afterwards, I received from Blumenbach an invitation to a ball for that evening.

My first personal contact was with my banker, a palmy tradesman, who, under the spur of hope from triple prospective profits through the conversion of notes into gold, gold into notes, and either into linens and woolens, was profuse of offers, of counsel, of topical knowledge ; and on the instant sallied forth with me to find me lodgings, which he did promptly in the Berkenbush House, No. 37, Weender Street.

In the evening at eight, I was dressed for the ball, and had but to cross the corridor from my chamber to enter the dancing-room ; for Madame Blumenbach, instead of cramping herself and her company by squeezing one hundred and fifty people into her own moderate house, had wisely hired the capacious quarters at the Crown Inn, for her entertainment. And so I made my *début* at the University of Goettingen very gayly at a dance, given by its most renowned professor.

Among my letters was one to the principal personage in the town. He was not the Prorector, nor any member of the Academic Senate. These high officials controlled the *materiel* and the discipline of the University. The personage of whom I speak supervised them. This delicate, preëminent, and invidious function had been recently created by the governments of Germany, for the purpose of stifling a spirit of liberalism, whereof alarming symptoms had appeared among the professors in many Universities. England's King being King of Hanover, some air of British freedom was breathed by the lungs of Goettingen, whereby this University had, in the first quarter of the present century, expanded to be the best endowed, and most liberally conducted, and the most numerously and variously frequented in Germany. This unique privilege of Goettingen — derived from her connection with England — having always been discreetly enjoyed by her professors, the new office was for her almost superfluous; and, but for the need of uniformity, she probably would have been spared the shame of its presence.

The gentleman (Herr von Laffert) who held this high post, was a widower with three pleasing, refined daughters, whose matron, Frau von Vedemyer, was the wife of the chief judge (*Kanzelley-director*) of the southern district of Hanover — a lady, intellectual, spirited, and graceful. At Blumenbach's ball these two families began their friendly attentions, which only ceased on the last hour of my stay in Goettingen, twenty months later.

On the following morning, I installed myself in the Berkenbush House, a student *in* Goettingen, by no means a student *of* the celebrated University. Between me and this quickening sun of intellectual warmth, there lay a cloud so black and thick, that, could I not disperse it, as hopelessly should I shiver in beamless shade, as would the soil of Hanover, should the solar orb stand still at the noon of night with the antipodes — the cloud, which at all times, in one or other form, impends lowering over human affairs, fuliginous, minatory, obstructive of success — the cloud of ignorance. I knew not twenty words of German. It being in the middle of a term, the best teacher, Professor Benecke, had not an hour disengaged, which was fortunate; for Benecke, practically and critically master of both languages, German and English, and a lively instructor, was by birth a Swabian, and had not, in a long residence at the more classical North, entirely effaced certain provincialisms of pronunciation, which it had been disloyal to lodge in the hospitable ear of a confiding stranger. Luckily, for those first decisive months, when the lingual sounds are by reiteration forever embedded in the larynx through the tympanum, I listened two hours daily, fore and afternoon, to the broad ultra-German tones of Dr. B., a Brunswicker, who gave especially the *eu* with such oily rotundity (delivering it like *awee* in English), that on my tongue he planted this important, ever-recurring vocalic compound in all its rich quality.

The Doctor was the only ass (pardon the bluntness of the word) I ever knew in Goettingen. Nor was he a learned ass, one of that laborious body of mental workers — from the facilities and cheapness of acquirement more numerous in Germany than elsewhere — who have the faculty to pile up facts without that of vivifying classification, who know how to accumulate intellectual coin but not how to spend it. The Doctor was, what is rare among the teachers of a German university, ignorant as well as dull. He was a man of about thirty, with a round face, glossy with health, and a continuous smile of contentment, and blessed with a patience that went hand in hand with his obtuseness.

He came honestly by his title. Whoever takes a degree — no difficult achievement — in any one of the four faculties of a German university, acquires thereby the title of Doctor, which he ever after wears through life, on all occasions, until he obtains a higher. This is the place to describe the academic organization. Laying aside, then, "Lessing's Fables," — which, with and without the Doctor, I worked into daily with a sudden German industry and doggedness, — let me endeavor, in few paragraphs, to give the reader a clear notion of what a German university is.

Yale and Princeton we call colleges; Harvard is a university, because here are the several series of professorships, with the requisite apparatus and facilities, which invite the graduates of colleges to enter on their professional studies, whether legal, theological, or medical. To perfect the claim of Harvard to the title of university — dispenser of all knowledges — she should have a fourth series (partially supplied by the lately established scientific school) embracing all the liberal studies not included in the other three, and called in Germany the faculty of philosophy. Such is the constitution of the German universities. There is no collegiate department. The preparatory studies are made elsewhere. Young men enter the university as ripe in years and acquirements as are our bachelors of arts, when, at the end of their senior collegiate year, they pass into the schools of law, medicine, or divinity. Nor is the German student under stricter discipline.

In Germany, the University is an institution of government, directly under the control of the state in whose territory it lies. The professors are appointed, and their salaries determined, by the state, which also establishes and appoints the academic regency, which, in Goettingen, consists of two bodies: a senate of about twenty members, and a university judiciary court, numbering nine or ten members, presided over by the Prorector.

So large and liberal was Goettingen in her plan and means, that she, above all other high academic institutions, deserved at that day the title of University. For, by the number and excellence of her teachers — not much short of one hundred — the wealth of her immense library (containing four hundred thousand volumes, and reputed the most complete in Europe), and the fullness of her adjuncts and auxiliaries, — museums, observatory, scientific gardens, — there was no recognized branch of knowledge in which, and at moderate cost, the most thorough instruction could not be obtained. In 1824, she counted among her professors, Blumenbach, Heeren, Eichhorn, Gauss, Langenbeck, Hugo, Ottfried Müller; and these, though having a European fame, were hardly more efficient as teachers than many others.

The number of professors with fixed salaries of from five hundred to twelve hundred dollars of our money was forty-five, distributed among the four faculties as follows: in the faculty of theology, five; of law, nine; of medicine, ten; of philosophy, twenty-one. Side by side with these salaried professors, there were (divided among the four faculties in similar proportions) an almost equal number of unsalaried private teachers, graduates of this or some other university, some of them superior men, retained or attracted by the resources of the library, the renown of Goettingen, and the consequent prospect of emolument or advancement. And finally, on the outskirts of this numerous diversified corps, supplying less essential educational wants, were riding-masters, music-masters, teachers of fencing, dancing, drawing.

A German professor is a hard worker. Some of those in Goettingen lectured two or three times daily for five days of the week, inspirited by the threefold stimulus of fame, money, and rivalry; for, besides the competition with colleagues, each professor has behind him one or more of the private teachers, licensed to lecture, and striving to come up with him, and fill a small auditorium by drafts from the larger one of his senior. A crowded lecture-room crowds the pocket, the fee from each student for a course (consisting of from forty to a hundred lectures) being a *louis d'or*, about four dollars. Several of the law professors had daily two hundred or more auditors for each of two or three courses, thus drawing from fees, in addition to salary, from four to six or seven hundred *louis d'ors* in one term, or from eight to fourteen hundred in the year; and as one dollar there goes further than two in America, a professorship in a prosperous German university may be one of the fattest offices in the kingdom or duchy.

In the summer term for 1825 there were in Goettingen fifteen hundred and forty-five students, apportioned as follows: theology, 310; law, 816; medicine, 217; faculty of philosophy, 182. The twenty-one professors of the last-named faculty would have had lean stalls, had their auditors been limited to the 182 enrolled on the catalogue as especially devoted to them. Scarcely a single student in the other three faculties but attended one or more of the courses in this miscellaneous department. Of these 1545 there were thirty-nine from Goettingen itself (the town had about 11,000 inhabitants), 699 from the kingdom of Hanover, and 807 from other parts of Germany and foreign lands. Among the foreigners were a Prince Suwarrow, grandson of the famous Russian Marshal; a Baron Oxenstierna, descended from the eminent Swedish Chancellor; three Brazilians, bearing the historical name of Albuquerque (one of whom was recently the minister from Brazil to the United States); and three Rothschilds, sons of the London Rothschild, the eldest of whom is the present Baron Lionel, the member elect of Parliament. Of the German students, fifteen were counts, and 227 of the inferior nobility with the title of *von*.

Here, then, were more than 1500 students and 100 teachers, making, of Goettingen, a circle of scholar-hives, the scholars swarming from morn till night in and out their cells to gather the honey of knowledge from the fluent lips of ripe professors, and, with their business, keeping the little town in a ceaseless hum. Among them I was a stranger, not permitted to work with them. In order that I may get power to do so, we must go back to "Lessing's Fables."

Unhappily for me, my Brunswick doctor had not read the "Vicar of Wakefield," or he might have profited by that genial gentleman's experience in teaching the Dutch English. In his un-German ignorance he understood but few words of French and not one of English. Sometimes, in my despair, while panting up the perpendicular steep of the German vocabulary, the happy Doctor, whom I engaged as a ladder, seemed more like an overhanging cliff baffling my endeavors. At the portal of the majestic golden palace of German thought, I beat for weeks, ere I could see any signs of the life within. Then, as if on a sudden, the doors swung open, and I had at first rapid glimpses, and then, in the shifting growing lights that filled the interior, broad sweeps and deep, tempting vistas.

The academic year is divided into two terms, or semesters, — a summer and a winter term, from

Easter to Michaelmas, and from Michaelmas to Easter, with two vacations of four or five weeks each between them. By working hard, that is, seven or eight hours a day, or half as much as a dutiful German dig, my ear had laid hold of so many word-laden sounds, and my understanding could extract the juice out of so many novel verbs and phrases, that, at the end of three months, I was ready to attend lectures, if not with the full profit of a native, with sufficient to reward the stretched attention, and with a daily enlarging sum of ideas taken in. By downright fagging and Teutonic tenacity (working right through the spring vacation), I had earned the key to all the treasures of Goettingen, and, to choose which should be opened first, I had only to inspect the *catologus prœlectionum publice et privatim in Academia Georgia Augusta per semestre œstivum A. CICICCCCXXIV. a die IV. majis habendarum.* Passing over in the catalogue the three finite faculties of theology, law, and medicine, and coming to the indefinite omnivorous faculty of philosophy, among whose twenty-one professors and their fifty-five subjects lay my choice, what a multitudinous, multifarious banquet was spread before me. History, ancient, mediæval and modern, general and particular; German literature, English, French, Spanish, Arabic, Judaic, Latin, Greek literature; logic; statistics; politics; æsthetics; mathematics; metaphysics; natural history; ethnography; mineralogy; physiology; archæology; mythology; geometry; political economy; public law.

From this distracting variety of intellectual cheer I selected for my first course — what, for one whose German dated from the end of January, would be the most readily digested — Heeren's modern history and his ethnography. In Goettingen each professor lectures in his own house. Behold me, then, on the fourth of May, 1824, with *mappe*, that is, portfolio to hold paper and pens, under my arm, on the way to the house of the celebrated Heeren, in the Pauliner Street, proud of, and eager to exercise, the new power of being a German auditor. The auditorium is furnished with benches and long narrow desks, just wide enough to support the student's portfolio. That of Heeren held about one hundred and twenty hearers. In the assigning of places, hospitality is practised toward strangers, those being given to them which are nearest the lecturer. Just before me was the counts' table, at which students with that title have the privilege of sitting, on payment of double fee. The room soon filled with young men whose average age was about twenty, well-looking, orderly, civil. Precisely at ten, Heeren entered, with a shrinking mien and rapid gait, as of a very shy man about to make his maiden effort at public speaking. His figure — somewhat above the middle height — was fleshy and ample without being heavy. His head and face were large, his kindly eyes light blue, his skin florid and transparent, his hair white, and his age about sixty. After some confusion and a feminine blushing diffidence, standing before his desk — placed in a corner on a platform a foot above the floor — he commenced as follows: "Gentlemen: for the advancement of the human race we should direct our aims particularly to those subjects which tend the strongest to a wholesome exercise and culture of the mind. Hence, natural sciences deserve our especial attention. Within the last century our knowledge of ethnography and geography has been much enlarged; and wars, which are so unfavorable to other branches of science and literature, have been one of the chief means of extending these two." Heeren's voice was distinct but weak, under effort or emotion running into falsetto. The moment he began, his words were accompanied by the sibilation of a hundred pens galloping over coarse paper. The lectures are delivered somewhat as a dictation, the speaker pausing often at the end of each sentence, longer than the repose of a period, to let the pens come up with him. By help of a little abbreviation, the fastest put down nearly every word he uttered. At ten minutes before eleven Heeren ceased speaking, and hastily gathering up his notes, hurried out of the room in the same crouching way that he had entered it, like a man escaping from oppressive approbation. The ten minutes are given, in order that students, who happen to have a lecture the next hour, may be punctual at another auditorium.

The theory of this lecture-and-note-system is, that before sleeping, the student applies, in the quiet of his room, more or less time to revising and conning his notes, so as to impress their substance and spirit on his mind while this is still malleable from the warmth of the professor's breath. But only the more thoughtful and methodical do their work with such thoroughness; and it is related of one who, after faithfully pursuing a long academic course, carrying away with him a score of bulky note-books, on the journey lost his trunk, which they half filled, and thus had to return to the university for another three years to retake the same notes. A fair satire on the abuse of copious lectures.

In the afternoon, I heard Heeren on modern history, from the end of the fifteenth century — to me the most attractive and instructive course that I attended while at Goettingen. When, after describing the breach between England and her American Colonies, he came to the Declaration of Independence, July 4th, 1776, his mind, swelling to the grandeur of the epoch, with solemn, agitated emphasis he concluded, *novus sæclorum nascitur ordo*. I, who had never heard or seen the name of Thomas Paine uncoupled with derision or scorn, looked up with a sudden surprise into the excited countenance of the professor, as he pronounced "Common Sense" the most important pamphlet in history. The younger Pitt was, as a statesman, the object, to him, of idolatrous admiration; and when he spoke of him as the chief of the coalition against France, his voice was almost choked by emotion.

With the opening of the new semester, I exchanged Dr. B. for Benecke, professor, librarian, and Hofrath (counsellor). Titles were thickly and acceptably strewn among the professors in Goettingen. Heeren, besides being Hofrath, was knight of the Order of Guelf. Against the assaults of any Swabian dissonances that still lingered in the throat of Benecke, I was shielded by the fortifications slowly but solidly built about my ears by my willing, patient Brunswicker. I was, moreover, additionally guarded by the instructions of Madame Vedemeyer and the Laffert ladies, natives of Celle, a small Hanoverian town, the Orleans of Germany, the one spot in all the broad Teutonic land where this great language is spoken in euphonious purity. In my visits — which I now wonder were not more frequent — these ladies notified me not only of Swabian trespasses, but of all the others whereof their noble tongue, in its manifold utterances, is the victim. They even cautioned me as to certain peccadilloes against the classical standard into which themselves had lapsed. To their other ladylike qualities, they added gentle voices, whose tones still live in my brain, a distinct musical memory.

Benecke was a strongly-marked character, energetic, decisive, one-sided — a man of the world, who conversed well and dressed well, and who piqued himself on his breeding; punctiliously polite to his equals, but curt and indifferent to those whose equality with himself was questionable. Toward a well-bred stranger he bore himself with an air which seemed to say, — "I am a gentleman, and you will have more pleasure in consorting with me than with most whom you will meet in these parts." Once, at an evening at Heeren's, he came to me with a flushed countenance and related in wrathful English (which he spoke without fault) how he had just been insulted by a Russian student, who asked at what hour he could give him a private lesson. The Hofrath wished, at such meetings, to sink the teacher, wherein he was right. I sympathized with him, though astonished at his taking the thing so to heart. With a little more of the Christian element in his gentlemanhood, he would, in his long experience, have discovered that, in their unavoidable and healthy rawness, the best-disposed among the young are liable to crimes against the *bienséances*, and that it takes years to polish even fine material into unfaltering propriety. Had he, interrupting the untimely applicant with a significant smile, said blandly in his ear, "Come to me to-morrow morning," the young man would have felt the rebuke and have profited more than by an indignant rebuff. We were always good friends; but yet I fear, over his memory of me, whenever, if ever, he thought of me, there passed a cloud; for, on his kindly coming to bid me farewell the day before I finally left Goettingen, on rising at the end of the visit, he so took me aback by expressions of thankfulness for my kindness to him, that I had nothing to say in return, and it was only after the door was closed that with mortification I perceived my seemingly heartless omission, as I recalled the blankness of his look at my silent, cool receptivity. It was another instance of form killing substance. His thanks to me were mere formality; mine to him would have been the cordial wording of a genuine gratitude for the much that I had learnt from him, and for his unbroken courtesy in a professional intercourse of more than two hundred hours.

In person, Benecke was every way large, being six feet high, broad, deep-chested and corpulent; yet moving at sixty with the easy spring of inward vigor. I took my lesson before breakfast, at six in summer and seven in winter, walking every morning to his distant house near the Groner Gate. He never failed to come in dressed, brushed, and shaved, with his capacious black frock-coat tightly buttoned over his abdomen — voluminous and warm with the best digestion of choice aliment — and his large, handsome, pulpy hand as well *soignée* as that of a Parisian *élégant.*

From the jump we went at *Nathan the Wise*, Lessing's masterpiece — pure hard German, a favorite with Benecke, whose clear understanding found in Lessing's artistic handling, clean humanity, and compact reason, a satisfactory substitute for poetry. With him I first opened the magic book of *Faust*, to wonder forever at the fantastic, weird scenes played on a ground of solid, burning reality; in their terrible power and beauty like the frenzied flames that shoot through the windows of an indestructible edifice, consuming in and about it whatever is perishable. Of course, by the strange novelty and material blaze was I first impressed; for only ripeness of experience in life and literature can pierce the subtlest irony that ever shone through words; can prize the exuberant variety, the divine naturalness, the brimming flow of deepest thought and feeling, so wonderfully matched with language; can fully enjoy the infallible art which draws a ravishing harmony out of discord and abruptest contrasts, making the fresh and guileless, like flowery tendrils overhanging a precipice, stand unconsciously, in fearful significance, beside the blasted and the tragic. After I had become intimate with modern German, Benecke persuaded me to make acquaintance with the ancient, and we went through together the shadowy, grand old Niebelungenlied. In the naif poetry — fragrant with morning's breath — of the twelfth and thirteenth centuries he so delighted, that he edited one of its long poems, "Wigalois," from the manuscript.

Benecke told me that Coleridge, when at Goettingen, toward the close of the last century, was an idler, and did not learn the language thoroughly, and that he got a long ode of Klopstock by heart and declaimed without understanding it, playfully mystifying his countrymen with the apparent rapidity of his progress. When the "Opium-Eater" appeared, Benecke at once attributed it to Coleridge, from knowing, he said, that Coleridge took opium when at Goettingen.

Promoted in my intellectual status in Goettingen, I also bettered my corporeal. The Berkenbush House, old, stale, and noisy, was good enough for a green beginner; but now that I was printed on the University Catalogue student in the faculty of philosophy, with all the privileges, opportunities, utilities, superiorities, prosperities of such, I wanted rooms more neat, sightly, and quiet. These I found in a newly-built, and, what was more important, freshly furnished house in a side-street, occupied by Municipal Senator Berg, with whom I was the only lodger. And here the reader, having now some insight into the mental life of a student in Goettingen, may desire to know about his bodily life and its cost.

For furnished lodgings he pays from two to ten dollars a month, two or three for a single room, four to six for two, and eight to ten for a suite of three. Breakfast is furnished, and also tea, if required, by the landlord at a stipulated price. For his dinner he sends to a *traiteur*, or dines at one of the hotels, the charge varying, according to quality, from three to ten dollars a month. Attendance, boots, and washing are all cheap, notwithstanding which I had a lawsuit with my washerwoman, whose bill, according to Goettingen tariffs, was on one occasion so impudently extortionate, that in disgust I refused to pay it. A few days afterwards, to my astonishment, a summons to the university court was served on me. To the astonishment of the washerwoman I obeyed the summons, instead of seeking a compromise. The judge, on glancing at the account, pronounced the sum total very high; whereupon the plaintiff, backed by several witnesses in petticoats, exclaimed on the immensity of the gentleman's weekly bundle, protesting that in it, besides endless other articles, were always seven shirts. Hereupon the judge looked at me expectantly, he and the clerk and the few persons present evidently awaiting an indignant denial of this accusation; and confident I am, that had I not been present to plead guilty by silence to the extraordinary charge, his Honor would have gravely warned the woman against the heinousness and perils of perjury. Nevertheless, she had to submit to an abatement of her account.

The average total annual expenditure of a native student is about three hundred dollars. Many spend more, a few much more, and some do with less than two hundred. An Englishman, after a short acquaintance with Goettingen, surprised at the cheapness, declared that, for one hundred pounds sterling, a man might live like a gentleman and keep a horse. From experience, I should say that his estimate supposes a minuteness of thrift inconsistent with the habits of one who indulges in so high a luxury.

A student's life depends as much on his mates as his masters. Only through companionship with equals can the young as well as adults grow healthfully. Seclusion curdles the blood. The advantage of schools and colleges is not more in the coöperation of many teachers than in that of many learners. These work together, and work upon one another. Sympathy and competition are light and air to the mind. Where these are not, there is the pallor and lassitude of darkness and stillness.

By companionship and collision the weak are strengthened, the strong tempered. At the universities some seem to be sacrificed; but, away from this crowd, would such weaklings have had the marrow to withstand other temptations?

A stranger arriving from Hanover on a sunny forenoon, and entering the Weender Gate, might infer, as he passed down the main street, that Goettingen was the seat of idleness and revelry; for at the corners, and lounging along the sidewalks, he would see scores of students: some with the unkempt, torpid look of a late beer-debauch, some with the saucy port of sword-skilled quarrellers, and all busy keeping their pipes on fire. A hundred or two of such give the small town an aspect of dangerous idleness. But, at the same hour, a thousand are eagerly gathering into their portfolios the sentences of a dozen lecturers, or silently bracing themselves by solitary study for the ordeal through which each one must pass to reach his chosen vocation; for, not only those destined to the three great professions, but all who aspire to any one of the various public employments, must submit to a searching examination by the state after undergoing the comparatively indulgent one of the university. And, moreover, many of these loungers and brawlers are rapidly sowing their wild oats, and will, some of them the very next semester, buckle to their desks with zealous, sober industry.

Duelling is one of the institutions of the German university. When the reader learns that, in Goettingen, in 1824, there were, on an average, two or three duels a week, he will understand that they were not combats *à l'outrance.* Students' duels are hybrids between a sham fight and a mortal encounter, compromises between honor and danger, a braggadocio mimicry of semi-barbarous mediæval manhood. In Goettingen the weapon is the straight double-edged sword, and thrusts are not allowed. The antagonists stand up, sword in hand, with seconds, witnesses, and surgeon ; but, against mortal or maiming wounds, the following are the provisions : a thick felt, intrenchable, broad-brimmed hat, an impenetrable stock well up on the chin, round the waist and abdomen, wadding impervious to steel, and the same for the sword-arm ; and, as a final shield, the sword of the second, who wards from his principal some of the worst blows. Ugly gashes are sometimes cut upon the face or breast ; but mostly these encounters end without bloodshed, after a certain number of rounds or of flat strokes. At times, but rarely, there is a meeting without hat or bandages ; and then mischief may be done by the weapons, in addition to that of expulsion.

The governments wink at the deathless duels, regarding them probably as safety-valves for the escape of the combative energies, which might otherwise take a more public direction. These martial masquerades busy the belligerent impulses, and flatter youth with the show of independence and manly freedom. For the culture of courage they are needless; for in this quality the Germans have ever been abreast of their bravest neighbors.

To return to the matter of companionship.

Where there is not (and there is nowhere) the freest play of the faculties and impulses, superficial attractions will often anticipate or supersede the deeper. Thus, at a crowded German university — like Goettingen in that day — in such repute as to draw to its halls from all the constituencies of the German confederation, the new-comers will feel irresistibly the drift of territorial attraction, and find themselves at once absorbed into *Landsmanschaften*, that is, organized unions of students from the same section or kingdom. When, in addition to geographical separation — and that far wider than any made by the conventional boundaries between conterminous homogeneous states — there is the still broader separation of language, the attraction of speech will in the beginning be paramount; and so, in the very first days, I found myself acquainted with several Britons — I say Britons, because of the Scotch, who came to study civil law, which is the basis of theirs. But I had not been many weeks in Goettingen, when there arrived a fellow-countryman, in whose mind and character I found that support and comfort which — especially in the remote isolation of a foreign land — make a friend so valuable. He is now a prosperous, honored gentleman,[1] having achieved in an arduous intellectual profession the esteem and success which surely attend ability, rectitude, and self-respect, even in a world where craft and shamelessness so often thrive. Of another fellow-countryman, long since deceased, I have a pleasant remembrance across the wide gulf of years, — Henry Dwight, the youngest son of the former eminent President Dwight, of Yale College. He came later to Goettingen, and stayed but a few months. Sprightly, sociable, and affectionate, on his honest, unconventional manners he wore that bloom which mantles on an incorruptibly moral nature, when united with joyous animal spirits. I introduced him at Madame Vedemeyer's, but neither family took to him, and he and Mr. Laffert — who of course was a high Tory — never failed, when they met, to get quickly into an exacerbating argumentation. Dwight would not purposely have hurt the feelings of a fly, and nevertheless one evening, when French, as usual, had been freely spoken round the room, he managed to announce, with animated emphasis, that never had he known a German who did not pronounce French abom-

[1] William Emerson, Esq., of New York; who has recently retired to his native town of Concord, Massachusetts.

inably. His own French was transparently Connecticutian.

Coupled with Dwight in my memory, is a distinguished English celebrity, Dr. Pusey, who accompanied him one day in a brief call at my rooms. He was a slight figure of medium height, with a thin face, exhausted by study. He worked, it was said, sixteen hours a day at German, whereby, at the end of six weeks, he had so far mastered the language as to be able, by limiting his application to the one branch, to read all German books on theology, the cream of which — so much of it as had risen in 1824–5 — he collected at the bookstores and carried away, to be digested in England, where, through the marvellous transformations and eliminations wrought by the cerebral chemistry, it was, some years later, precipitated from his brain in the form of "Oxford Tracts."

Three or four of my readers may have had in their hands a book with the following title: "The Metaphysic of Ethics; by Immanuel Kant. Translated out of the original German, with an introduction and appendix, by J. W. Semple, Advocate. Edinburgh: 1836." This gentleman, among my earliest acquaintance in Goettingen, was the first person who ever talked Kant to me, and that in very brief chapters, owing to the then metaphysical inappetency of his hearer. He was a short alert young man, with a quick eye and lively countenance, — a vivacious talker. He told me that while studying Kant he became so absorbed, that once he did not breathe out-door air for three weeks; and that when he came again upon external nature, the whole aspect was changed — with so new, and so transfiguring a mental vision had Kant endowed him. That he was worthy to interpret the deep Königsberg thinker, whoever will read the above stout volume will be convinced.

That there was in Goettingen no theatre, was to me a double deprivation — of amusement and of instruction. A crabbed old Count, who, not being a reading man, was, for the good of his student-sons, suffering in the not over-clean little town, the longings and *ennuis* of exile, on somebody deploring this want, rejoined, "If you have no theatre, you have a capital comedy." "Where?" "Blumenbach's lectures on natural history."

The renowned Blumenbach, one of the first of naturalists, was, moreover, one of the best of story-tellers, and enlivened and, as he said, impressed his lessons in natural history by numerous anecdotes, related with sly humor and an artistic comic dryness, his shrewd, wrinkled countenance of seventy summers, playing in the performance an harmonious, effective part. The coming joke announced itself by a roguish smile that took possession of his expressive mouth. In speaking of the whale, after a slight premonitory pause, he would proceed with a gravity that would have entrapped a novice: "God forbid, gentlemen, that I should trench upon the domain of my esteemed co-laborers of the theological faculty, but the history of Jonah having lived three days in a whale's belly laps over into my province; and after a conscientious scrutiny of this eccentric event, the only explanation that I can give of it is, that Jonah, in his travels, was by stress of funds obliged for that number of days to put into a roadside inn with the sign of the whale." To exemplify the sagacity of the dog, he related that an eminent surgeon of Paris, having taken into his study a pet quadruped of a friend, to cure it of a broken leg, some days after he had sent the dog home cured, he heard a scratching at the door, on opening which, there was his late patient, who, with affectionate wagging of tail, smiled up into his face, distinctly asking a like benefaction for a brother poodle with a broken leg, whom he had brought with him. Whether or not the relater himself believed the story, it would have puzzled the most sagacious physiognomist to discover.

In Blumenbach's teaching there was profit, not merely from the fulness and completeness of his knowledge, but from his lucid method in delivering it. His understanding was compact and singularly clear, and there was in him that healthy tone which a life-long zealous study of nature imparts to a capable mind. In his speech and manners he had the gentleness and friendliness which confidential intercourse with the quiet beneficent phenomena of creation had cultivated, if not engendered; for he was by nature a naturalist. In figure he was about the average size, neither slight nor stout, of such a build and organization that his person were best described by saying that it was not corporeal. He took pleasure in conversation, and besides the evening when, in Madame Blumenbach's drawing-room, by them and their daughter visitors were cordially welcomed, he would readily in the day give audience in his study, enjoying much the visits of strangers, particularly those of British breed, for which he had a not intolerant partiality. On those occasions he was communicative and instructive, and most affable. In the summer of 1825 I took to see him an intelligent Scotch gentleman, an acquaintance I had made at Weimar. Blumenbach, with amiable pride — for he was honorably alive to evidences of his wide reputation — called our attention to the gem of his collection, sent to him from Edinburgh by, I think, Sir William Hamilton — a cast from the skull, just discovered, of Robert Bruce, the most remarkable feature in which, he thought, was the great strength and depth of the lower jaw-bone.

He led us into his cabinet of crania, and described the ecstasy of Gall, many years before, in the outset of his investigations, on first beholding it.

Blumenbach, of a somewhat timid nature, was at fifty too old to accept a discovery so immense and startling as that by Gall of the physiology of the brain; and therefore to him even his own precious collection was but dead bones in comparison to what it was to the creative, life-breathing insight of Gall.

My friend was charmed with his visit to Blumenbach, and, if still alive, will recollect a remark which the kindly old man made as we were on our legs to take leave of him, namely, that no day passed without adding to his knowledge. For him, life at threescore and ten had not lost its saltness, which it does lose for whoever, at whatever age, ceases to learn.

A compeer of Blumenbach in age and reputation was Eichhorn. I did not attend his lectures, which were exegesis of different books of the Old Testament; but I paid him from time to time a Sunday visit (Sunday was the day for morning visits in Goettingen), and I was occasionally a guest at his hospitable suppers, at one of which, sitting next to his son, then an eminent professor of law, and since one of the cabinet ministers of the King of Prussia, he inquired about our law studies in America; and on my telling him that our basis is the common law of England, and that we begin with Blackstone's Commentaries, he startled me by expressing his surprise that a book so superficial should be made so much of in England and America. There was a piece of information to be casually picked up at the highest seat of learning in Germany.

The elder Eichhorn, the redoubtable rationalist commentator, who, in his handling of Isaiah or Moses, cut sacrilegiously through the adipose deposits of tradition, was in figure inclined to rotundity; as though in the excessive sedentariness of his life — sitting fifteen or sixteen hours a day at his desk — his flesh stagnated about his bones. His face, in its expression, but not in its mould, intellectual, was sallow and fleshy, and lighted by a dark eye full of life, which contrasted well with his thick white hair, combed up and back from his not high forehead. In spite of his fifteen studious hours, and by virtue of the extreme regularity in all things of the habits of most German professors, he had good health. One day a friend finding him unwell, and asking the cause of this rare interruption to his ordinary condition, with self-reproach he replied, "Yesterday I was fool enough to go and take a walk." He was now past seventy, and in 1825 I witnessed the torchlight procession of the students who came under his windows to do him honor on the fiftieth anniversary of his professorship. It would not be easy to forget the kind, almost affectionate greeting this venerable scholar would rise to give me on my visits. With amiable interest he would ask about my studies, and the lectures I attended. When I told him that I heard no metaphysics — "In that you do well," he said. "Metaphysicians busy themselves with questions they can never solve — the essence of the mind and soul, the freedom of the will, immortality. What can we ever know about these?" Herein he betrayed the limitations of his own nature. The widest and most aspiring minds will, and by their very breadth and loftiness, must put such questions, and will have answers to them; and when they cannot discover the answers, will invent such as shall be makeshifts while awaiting the discovery, which, too, they indirectly accelerate by agitating, animating, oxygenating the world's intellectual atmosphere. The great themes they deal with are accessible and soluble; but their method being purely speculative, and therefore one-sided and not truly scientific, they reach no solution, even through the flashings of intuition. But these flashings, if not warm enough for solvents, are enough so for watch-fires. The one-sidedness of the metaphysician comes not entirely from a preponderance of the ratiocinative intellect, but in part from deficiency in the emotive element. He is too cold for discovery. From being subsympathetic it is that the metaphysician is supersensuous and supersubtle; and hence his subtlety is apt to overshoot the mark and drive on to vacuity. The ingenious threads he spins, attenuated by intellectual over-action, wanting the staple of sensibility, grow too fine to bind any thing.

Not much the junior of Eichhorn was Bouterwek, still an active laborer, lecturing on logic, ethics, æsthetics, literature. But though, from the extent and variety of his literary learning, he had a European name, his not being a mind of original power or genial insight, he had in a degree outlived his reputation. To me, in my novitiate, his course on German literature was valuable. I still see the rather small head and face of the gentle old man bent over his notes, from which he looked up now and then to say his best things; and I still, with a mingled feeling of compassion and amusement, hear him, when speaking of the Schlegels, with a surprising *naïveté*, and in a tone half imploring, half protesting, wonder why these gentlemen let slip no opportunity of laughing at him. It might have been whispered in his ear, that the Schlegels — neither the most generous nor the most profound of men — enjoyed the triumph of prosaic, selfish natures in being able effectively to ridicule one who, with a wide fame, was still less profound than themselves.

On the list of professors in the faculty of philosophy, the closing name, because the last appointed, was that of Ottfried Müller, then apparently not more than thirty years of age, a man of rare promise, which the shortness of his life alone prevented from being fulfilled. Of his thorough knowledge of Greek life and nature I had the benefit as a hearer of his course on ancient art. This course was delivered in one of the public halls, where was the collection of casts from the antique, which were to me the occasion of a daily-repeated disappointment, my expectation that he would turn to these inspired models of beauty, and through them make his lessons emphatic by practical comment, being every day baffled to the very end of the course.

The lectures of Sartorius I did not hear, because with his rival, Saalfeld, I was from the beginning drawn into the only intimate personal relations that I had with a professor. Between these two there was no love lost; nor generally was this divine virtue more dominant in the hearts of Goettingen's teachers than in those of men less intellectualized. In its learned supremacy, the university found not a whit more exemption from envy and jealousy than does a worshipful bench of bishops in its lordly preëminence. The conditions are as yet nowhere compassed for that perfect moral contentment and inviolate Christian good-will, to be bred from the complete fulness of outward and inward activity — a fulness solely attainable through the rule of laws, social and industrial, far deeper than have yet been obeyed. Thence, although science, letters, culture are humanizing and refining, nevertheless, the strata of society, which, through knowledge and privilege of opportunities, are the superior, are liable like the others to be invaded and stained by fire-driven "dykes," and to be otherwise disturbed or dislocated, or, in geological phrase, made "unconformable" by the action of the central heats, which can, through these laws only, be disciplined and harmonized without loss of vivifying force. The professors were not at all a mutual-admiration-society; and to hear the full music of praise, which so many of them merited, it was necessary to get away some distance from Goettingen.

Sartorius, besides being a well-qualified teacher, deserved to have Americans among his hearers, were it only for one opinion uttered by him in his course on politics, viz., that the most instructive reading on this subject are the speeches in the United States Congress. His rival, Saalfeld, was a much younger man, being not over forty, and one of the hardest workers in a numerous company of fourteen-hour men. Every day he lectured on politics, on the history of Europe since the beginning of the French revolution, on political economy, and three times a week on the law of nations, besides, on Saturdays, a *collegium practicum diplomaticum*, a class for exercises in public law; all of which courses, during my three semesters, I attended. When two lectures followed one the other, snatching his watch he would run up from the lecture-room into his study, quickly light a pipe, ever and anon intermitting the hasty puffs to diversify the nicotine stimulant with sips of strong hot coffee, thus making the most, as he thought, of the ten minutes' interval, to fortify his brain for the second labor. For some time, we dined together at the public table of the *Stadt-London* Hotel. After the thin daily soup, he would mix a spoonful of French mustard with oil, vinegar, pepper, and salt, as a sauce to replace the flavor the daily boiled beef had tried to give the soup. The gradation of his appetite, in the opening week of a semester, was an instructive hygienic phenomenon. Languid during the vacation, with the first lecture it would quicken, with the second get to a brisk trot, until, by the end of four or five days, when all his courses had got under way, it would grow to a vigorous gallop, to which it held till the next vacation, only slackening into a quiet canter on Sundays.

Saalfeld, mobile, excitable, was in temperament more Gallic than German. In stature he was of medium size and make, nervous and fleshless, with a good expanse of forehead, a restless eye that shone through spectacles, and a countenance whose expression, by aid of a wide, intellectual mouth, shifted with singular rapidity from grave to gay. On a good, virile, unhesitating voice, he ascended at times in his lectures to strains of eloquence. He was a bachelor, and many a pleasant evening have I spent with him. To each new-comer, he would present a fresh clay-pipe, with the smoker's name on the bowl of it, and after smoking put it away on a triangular shelf in one corner, so that each guest would find, on returning, the same pipe. In conversation he was various and rapid, and, when speaking of pretenders and shams, could be satirical without malignity. He rarely went out, but he did me the favor to come to my rooms one evening to drink some Tokay, sent me after his return home by a Polish fellow-student to whom, in his republican enthusiasm, I had given my copy of the Federalist. I was occasionally a guest at dinners or suppers — Mr. Laffert being the principal dinner-giving host. Saalfeld would rally me about those entertainments, where the company consisted almost exclusively of professors; and when I would affirm that I found them very pleasant, he would rejoin: "My dear sir, I will prove to you that they *must* be stupid. Our professors keep all their good things for their books or lectures, and are especially careful not to let any of them escape in presence of their colleagues, lest these should steal them; which they certainly would. You will not tell me that any of them are so rich as to have wit to spare for their neighbors." With much *gusto*, imitating the swollen tone in which his accomplished colleague at times enveloped his sentences, he would tell of an interview which Sartorius was said to have once had with the Emperor Alexander. By one of the smaller German States, or by several of the smallest united, Sartorius had been sent as envoy to the Congress of Vienna in 1815. One day the Emperor of Russia took him aside, and with earnestness, thus addressed him: "Mr. Sartorius, what busies and weighs on my mind, day and night, is, to discover the means whereby I can best advance the welfare of my subjects. Having in your knowledge and judgment the utmost confidence, I address myself to you, to learn by what course of policy, by what principles and institutions, I can best attain my end?" "Sire," replied Sartorius, "beyond measure am I rejoiced that your Majesty is possessed by such noble desires, and most happy that I can repay your Majesty's confidence, by informing you where you can learn all that you need to carry into effect your exalted purpose." "Where, my good friend, where?" exclaimed the Emperor with eager attention. "Sire, study my works." What the story had gained by the absence of that charity before alluded to, I cannot decide.

I once said to Saalfeld, so saturated had I become with the learned effluvia of Goettingen, I felt that I, too, should have to write a book. The remark was the most groundless, momentary, playful invention, not having the tiniest fibre of a root in any incipient desire, presentiment, or most shadowy literary dream, and had any one then told me that such would yet be my fate, I should have stared with as perfect an incredulity as does the veriest low-browed urchin when rebuked with the warning that he will one day come to the gallows. Saalfeld replied: "I will let you into the mystery of authorcraft. Books are now written by machinery." "By machinery?" "Yes; the important thing is, to get the right machine, which I will describe to you. It consists of eight or ten narrow shelves, three or four feet long, movably hung round a circular skeleton four feet in diameter, so as always to preserve the perpendicular position when the frame to which they are attached is turned by a crank. This shelf-armed machine, loaded with books, on the proposed subject, selected from the library, is placed beside the author's table. Without stirring, he brings to his eye row after row of the most choice material methodically arranged, and, with his pen in one hand and the crank in the other, he sets vigorously to his task, and the crank does the best of the work. Beside his desk every one of us has a machine of this structure." Similar in purport to Saalfeld's fun, was the fling, from a teacher in a rival university, at Goettingen, whose professors, he said, were mushrooms that grew along the walls of the library. One day, toward the close of the summer semester of 1825, — my last — speaking of degrees, he proposed to me that I should take one and become a doctor of philosophy. "Is it so easy to be obtained?" I asked. "Nothing easier. You have only to choose one of the subjects on which you have heard lectures with me — public law, for instance — and I will prepare you in three weeks to pass the examination. I guarantee your honorable passage through. The most puzzling question that will be asked you will be: 'Have you, sir, in your pocket, thirteen *louis d'ors* for the University treasurer?'" The proposal was tempting — *doctor philosophiæ:* a degree from the great University of Goettingen. But the temptation lost daily of its charm. Such doctors were plenty in those latitudes. Had the dry parchment cost only the three weeks' dry work, it had been well. But the thirteen *louis d'ors;* gold grows daily heavier in the last weeks of a student's career. I kept the *louis d'ors* in my pocket, to be less dryly spent, and left Germany without a title.

Poor Saalfeld! His end was sad. More true to his liberal principles than so many who are only brave in words, with all the vivacity of his excitable temperament, he threw himself, in 1830, into the revolutionary movement consequent in Germany on the expulsion from France of the elder Bourbons. The anxieties of such an undertaking, quickly followed by its failure, overtasked a highly nervous organization. His intellect became unsettled, and, in that melancholy state, he died. He was a generous, high-spirited man, and, in the palmy days of Goettingen, one of her most brilliant lecturers. In Germany and in other lands, his memory is still affectionately and respectfully cherished by the survivors of the many who profited by his conscientious, able, and zealous teachings.

VII.

My First Vacation.

AT the end of my first semester in 1824, I had earned the autumn vacation. For more than seven months, without flagging, without regaling myself with the intermittence of a single unbusied day, I had digged and wrought at the soil of Teutonic speech, which already for some moons had gratefully yielded me of its fruit, and more ripely with each successive week. I had got to feel at home in my seat under the lecturer's desk. Sounds at first harsh had grown musical through meaning. The mysteries of German thought were unveiling themselves, and German ways had ceased to be strange to me. I was entitled, and in a certain degree prepared, to enjoy and profit by a short tour of travel and a visit to some of the capitals of Germany.

In our interchange of letters it was agreed with my uncle that we should make an excursion together, he timing his departure from Antwerp so as to reach Goettingen on the last day of the term, which he accordingly did with my aunt on the 12th of September. He travelled post in a spacious barouche, which made easy room for three and a servant, and all the luggage; for my uncle and aunt, being accomplished travellers, knew how to limit themselves in what the Romans felicitously termed *impedimenta*, and my one modest trunk added little to the bulk. The attendant was not of that fussy, ostentatious, independent, often costly and arbitrary class called *couriers*, but was a quiet, obedient, solid and somewhat stolid Flemish house-servant, whose chief defect was his weight of two hundred pounds.

Eastward was our course, and starting on Monday the 13th of September, an hour after noon, we ate at Muehlhausen our first supper — a meal not for a continent vegetarian, but for a carnivorous, luxurious, travel-whetted trencher-man, its chief virtues manifesting themselves in tender beefsteak and tenderer partridge, for which a fast of eight or nine hours had so attempered my young teeth that I astonished myself — not to speak of spectators — with an almost Tantalian insatiableness of appetite. Through the law whereby our doings are all inwoven into the texture of our being, I summon that supper to my mental presence distinctly to-day. The hint given by these far-snatched recollections may teach how animal indulgences that violate the higher nature, may not only outlive the body they flattered, but that, when our clay shall have re-mingled with the earth we have left, how they may sharpen themselves into spiritual stings. But that supper was guiltless; for every mouthful — so many as they were, — of partridge and steak went honestly and directly, without obstructive or malignant delays, to the building up of wasted tissue.

The road from Muehlhausen to Gotha was beautiful with hills and woods and valleys and peopled landscape, across which through the glistening noon hastened at times the transmuting shadows of happy clouds, sailing sunlit aloft. Did the reader ever reflect on the wind, what it is and what it does? See it hug that towering tree, in its invisible mighty arms folding the whole bulk of branches, which rebound from the embrace refreshed and cleansed and strengthened, the green world of leaves rustling with the life and joy of the heavenly osculation. This is a type of the wind's great office: it purifies and vivifies; it sweeps round the globe sweetening the breath of every thing that breathes; it is the soul of the air which, stagnant without it, corrupt and dead, were poisonous to plant or animal. Fellow-worker with the Sun, the vast vapor which he daily fabricates from the ocean, it wafts into the heart of continents, bringing to all that lives a first element of life — the living water.

The middle of September was too late for one of the most beautiful sights in rural nature — a broad level expanse of golden grain, broken into rolling waves by the caressing breeze. Nor had we the grand symphony of a gale, shaking the limbs of stoutest oaks as easily as a child its rattle, and verifying that fine imaginative stroke of Wordsworth, when he speaks of his favorite grove,

> "Tossing in sunshine its dark boughs aloft,
> *As if to make the strong wind visible.*"

In Gotha there is not much to delay the traveller. The Ducal Palace, from the absence of all æsthetic quality, is displeasing to the eye, and at first equally so to the thought, from the reflection, how disproportionately to the means of the tax-paying population the huge pile must have weighed for its construction, and continue to weigh for its maintenance, upon so petty a domain. But you soon discover that under its ample roof it harbors a Museum of Natural History, and Cabinets of Medals and Coins and Engravings, and a Picture-Gallery, and a Library of a hundred and fifty thousand volumes. The Gallery was evidently not much visited, and it was pleasant to witness the satisfaction of the courteous superintendent at having the opportunity to exhibit his treasures — which were, however, not of the most costly — and his growing complacency as he discovered in my uncle a full appreciator of his favorites — chiefly of the Dutch and German schools.

After tea we went to what was called the *Shoot-*

ing-House, where, on a large covered platform, scores of panting couples, apparently of mingled ranks, were spinning interwoven cycloids of waltz. Of all dances the waltz is the most seductive, to performers if not to spectators. In its twofold circling it embodies the combined movement of planetary circumvolution, each couple revolving on its own axis while playing in a wide orbit in time with cognate companions, the gravitation common to all being toward connubial humanity. This symbolic mystic quality gives it a unique attractiveness, and mysteriously heightens its grace and beauty, wherein it is as much superior to other dances as an English park with its flowing lines is to a French one with its rectilinear plantations. The pairing, with relative independence of other pairs on the floor, typifies hymeneal union, which is still more pointedly prefigured in the semi-embrace of each couple, — a proximity which, in our country at least, debars some of the more frugal and delicate-minded maidens from the fascinating vortex, in addition to those who are withheld by the nay of the soberer class of mammas. Extra turns, as they are called, being one of the courtesies of the floor, and any gentleman being therefore privileged to whirl away from her partner any lady who accepts the invitation, (and good reasons must be given for refusal,) you have in this erratic proceeding another prefiguration of what matrimonial partnership is liable to, the waltzing encompassment, having possibly first enkindled the illegal elective affinity.

Against the frowns of moralists, the stings of satire, the fulminations of the pulpit, the waltz has, in America, as well as in England, simply by its intrinsic resources, successfully battled its way into general practice, if not into universal favor. At one of our frequented sea-shore summer resorts, in the height of the season, the clergyman of a fashionable church levelled against it a sermon, deliberate, unsparing. One among the parents present — a gentleman refined, undemonstrative, considerate — rose in the middle of the discourse, and with his family left the church. What *he* had permitted to his daughters he would not sit and hear rebuked as an impropriety. Several young ladies, having often in conscious innocence joined in the waltz, uttered on coming out warm indignation; for to them the words from the pulpit came freighted with personal insult. I did not hear the sermon, but from the repulsion caused in some who did, and from what was said of it by others, the speaker had evidently not approached his audience from the right point. He had strung together the easy words of common-place denunciation, and, as much by shallowness as harshness, had with his first sentences wounded heathful sensibilities, smiting coarsely right upon the self-love of his hearers instead of appealing unassumingly to their self-respect, coldly casting his condemnation over them as an empowered superior, instead of gaining their ears through the irresistible solicitations of fraternal sympathy.

Some preachers would do quite as well to hurl from the pulpit billets of wood at their parishioners as the words sometimes thrown out, so lifeless are these, so blockish, so unsympathetic, and at the same time so dictatorial, and thence so irritating and obnoxious. A kindly, tender, simple, not over-colored setting forth of the danger to modesty and maidenly reserve through the contacts of the waltz, a brotherly suggestion of what need there ever is of parental dutifulness, and still more of self-watchfulness, in order that the fires within the human breast, kindled there by God, to warm and illume the world, burn not profanely but always holily, — a premonition in this tone might have wrought upon the father, (whom the opposite one had offended,) to reconsider his parental permission; and, through the feelings awakened in the ingenuous girls, might have alarmed their modesty, and upon all present have produced a sound restraining effect.

The waltz, as miscellaneously practised, is a questionable indulgence, not to refined young women merely, but to both sexes; for young men may, and often do, enter the world with feelings as chaste as those of unspotted well-guarded girls, and with a profound boundless respect for the other sex, especially for its purity. These feelings should, in opening life, be carefully cherished on both sides; for, although to the pure all things are pure, some conditions and conjunctions being hostile to continued purity, the whitest may, insensibly to themselves, in certain exposures, become soiled; and where there is on one side callow innocence and on the other polished sensuality, the ingenuous may receive a taint of which the feelings will not in all cases be readily disinfected. What can be said positively is this: — there would be no harm in angels waltzing.

From Gotha to Weimar was a sunny mid-day drive of five hours. To travellers the theatre is always a post-prandial resource. The Diary has no note, nor have I any recollection of what we saw there; but whatever it was, it gave occasion, between my uncle and me, to a discussion on the Unities, sentences whereof might have been heard by Goethe, had he been on the alert, for in high talk we passed under his windows on our way back to the hotel; and as Goethe had the faculty of feeding his wisdom from the utmost variety of food, and could, with his genial power of appropriation, draw drops of nourishing juice out of fragments and driest or crudest material, he might have caught a breath of profit from the flitting discussion. The disputants did not go far into principles; for that they were both too inexpert. My uncle, though master of English, had not mastered Shakespeare. His notions on dramatic models were drawn from the practice of Corneille and Racine, and the interpretations of Boileau. My citadel was Shakespeare, and from the sallies I attempted to make into the enemy's lines, I quickly fell back upon him, finding that the most efficient weapons my adolescent tongue could wield were his example and towering success. At that time I had not studied his pages, and had only partially read them — in so far as any one can be said to read Shakespeare without studying him. But I knew that he was a mighty power, and the unhewn argument I drew from his splendid practice was enough to hold me unharmed against an opponent who was not strongly founded in poetic principles nor overskilled in critical dialectics.

On the sixteenth we made a long day from Weimar, through Naumburg and Lutzen to Leipzig, whose plains have been martial arenas where with the sword mighty causes were tried. When these encounters have possession of the mind the one man who haunts the imagination is the great Swede — truly a king among men — Gustavus Adolphus. Him in his heroic stature, we look up at, the heart heaving with high emotion as we gaze and spring toward a nature so noble and commanding.

After a three days' carnage Napoleon fled beaten and baffled from the field of Leipzig which, considering the hundreds of thousands engaged, and the vastness and complication of the interests dependent, was one of the critical battles of history. *Voelkerschlacht* the Germans name it, — Battle of the Nations, — so many, nearly all indeed, of the States of Europe being there represented on one or the other side. Had Napoleon been victor at Leipzig, there had been no Waterloo. But sooner or later he was doomed to be crushed; for his godless mind, lacking all sense of humility and moral limitation, aimed at material heights forbidden to man; *his* will, not divine will, being to him the law supreme. He was a gigantic practical blasphemer.

Leipzig, now a city of one hundred thousand souls, counted then but thirty-five thousand. Through beautiful shaded paths and gardens I walked nearly round it, and then from the top of the Observatory had a wide view, including the whole battle-field. The streets were big with the coming fair. But the principal events of my one day in Leipzig were scholarly. There is a custom in Germany — a generous duteous custom, significant of the largeness and free munificence of letters — whereby elevated teachers and men of learning or literature lay themselves open to all who wish to come within the personal sphere of their light. You need no voucher or introduction, but go up to the door and knock. You are received with an easy welcome, with a manner which says, 'I expected you, and am happy to see you.' The intellectual magnates of the land keep open hall, and any one who knows them to be such, or is in any degree capable of enjoying their high hospitality, is welcomed and entertained.

On the University advertisement I found the names of the Professors of History, (that being the subject with whose vocabulary my ear was most intimate,) and their hours of lecturing; and after listening to two of them in the *auditorium* penetrated to the *sanctum*. In the morning I heard and visited Professor Wieland, who on that day happened to be biographical, and thence the more attractive, sketching Francis I., Maria Theresa, Frederick the Great, and Joseph I.; and in the afternoon Professor Beck on the Seven Years' War. As the forenoon lecturer had touched on this famous conflict, and it had of course a place in Heeren's modern history, which I had just been attending, the kindly old gentleman laughed heartily when on my return to Goettingen I related to him my lecturing adventures in Leipzig, with the double repetition of the Seven Years' War.

Starting from Leipzig at eight in the morning, we fell short of Dresden, and made our evening halt at Meissen, which was a long posting-day from Leipzig, entering the capital on Sunday morning the nineteenth.

Dresden is a rich heiress, her heritage being picture-galleries and artistic collections bequeathed by some of her former sovereign fathers, to whom, by stranger as well as native, rare honor be given, that their royal wills were subject to such noble preferences. Many objects in several of the collections are more curious, from manipulating skill and eccentric fancy, than æsthetically satisfying; but the picture-gallery is one of the finest in Europe, and the cabinet of engravings is unique in its fulness and excellence.

To me, Dresden is memorable, that there I first beheld a King. A King! What an endless invisible line of kings; of kings read of, kings fancied, kings stowed in the ambitious memory innumerable, kings exalted, bedecked by juvenile imaginations, — a line stretching back into the cloud-lands of history, through all ages and countries, was now to terminate in visible anatomic actuality, expectation being exasperated by a lifelong transatlantic remoteness from all regal presence, and only tantalized occasionally by begilded counterfeits on the stage. My uncle was too workmanlike a traveller and active sight-seer to let opportunities escape; so an hour after our arrival we found ourselves stationed in the gallery through which the royal family passes on its way from the palace to the Catholic Church. Soon there were signs of the coming. Of what a trial he was about to abide; of what multifarious prefigurement his moving person was going to be the consummation; of the republican eyes, as yet virgin of royalty, eagerly set for him; of all this totally unconscious, on came his Saxon Majesty, Augustus III. An angle near where we stood shut us off from the royal party until it was close upon us: — and there at last was a King, an old man, "a fine respectable-looking man," says the Diary, dressed like other men, wearing no insignia except, I think, a broad blue ribbon across his breast. From the old King my eyes were soon diverted to one of the oung Princesses, with a pretty, happy face.

The King gave r a new sensation — no triumphant performan , when the subject is a youth not much out of his teens. Some days after I in return gave him one; and as he was in his seventy-second year, that was a satisfaction which probably neither courtier nor subject could have afforded him.

It was then a custom for the royal family, when at the summer-palace in Pilnitz, to dine on certain days in public; that is, into a gallery overlooking the dining-room spectators were admitted, tickets being issued by the proper official. Historic antiquaries probably know the origin of the custom. At the appointed hour, (a wholesome early one if I remember right,) we, with a few other excessive naturalists, were seated in the predominating gallery, and in a few moments the regal party, about a dozen in number, entered and took their seats with the unceremonious ease of well-dressed citizens around a family dinner-table. Persons royal being objects of everybody's knowledge, we upstairs were acquainted with the company below, while they knew no more of us than that we were individuals selected for over-curiosity. I think, by the by, that had I been at the table I should have had a prepossession against my over-lookers as a prying vacant rabble, who had nothing better to do than to spend time in seeing other people eat. It was, at all events, proper — being congregated together in the banquet-hall — that they at the table should on their side be made acquainted with us. Accordingly by the plate of the King was laid a list of all the spectators, made out with police-particularity, country, profession, age of each one being given. The ethnographic bill of fare may have been assistant to the culinary, causing a slight mental movement, and thus sharpening the relish of the soup, the nationalities of the gazers acting as a gentle excitant upon the palates of the tasters. Through the means of this form of presentation we partook somewhat of the character of spectatorial envoys. When the King came to *Americain* his Majesty ejaculated, *Mon Dieu!* and cast his royal eyes up to the gallery, expecting doubtless to recognize the American by his skin. This movement was followed all round the royal board, and the disappointment was probably general that among the lookers-on above there was neither a red man nor a black man.

When you consider the interior geographical remoteness of Dresden, that in 1824 there was neither locomotive nor steamboat in Germany; that during the Napoleonic wars few Americans travelled in Europe; that at that time we never had been diplomatically represented at Dresden; it may be honestly inferred that his Saxon Majesty had never consciously looked on a citizen of the United States, and therefore, that I was as novel a sight to him as he was to me, and thus that on the score of new sensations the Democrat and the King were quits.[1]

The picture-gallery was to my uncle a pasture glistening every morning with the dew of fresh beauties. By his side I walked a somewhat wilful colt. Not always duly considering the difficulty to the young æsthetic stomach of digesting large and

1 This was written before the publication of Washington Irving's *Life and Letters*, where we learn that in 1822 he spent several months at Dresden, and was a frequent guest at the palace. As one swallow does not make a summer, one American, even one so attractive and distinguished as Mr. Irving, could hardly have been sufficient to impress the notion of American nationality upon the brain of the sluggish old King; so that although the sensation I gave him was not a virgin one, it was akin to that, just as second love is sometimes almost as warm as first.

frequent meals of such concentrated food, my uncle would be piqued and disappointed if I at times grew wearied and restless, when his mature and practised faculties were still unsatisfied. Nature and instinct were, however, trusty guides to me; for in all forms and degrees of education, from the infantine primary to the virile academic, it is bootless to load the memory or perception with quantity or kind which the intellectual or sympathetic curiosity cannot appropriate.

Among the collections of Dresden, is one of antique marbles, a chaos of fragmentary reliques of ancient sculpture, limbs and heads and torsos and mutilated bodies, — marbles which have some value to the graduated connoisseur, and more to the professional student who has no access to the most inspired remains of ancient genius; but which, to the freshman in Art, have little other than the momentary interest derived from their antiquity. Ere the learned *cicerone* — whose tongue had never been cleansed by the benediction of brevity — got half through his biographico-critico-æsthetic exposition, I was jaded, and had I been obliged to follow him to the end, should, long before he reached it, have begun to wish that at sunrise he had been made to swim the Elbe haltered with the heaviest of his treasures.

The Greeks (and ancient sculpture though dug up at Rome is all Greek) were predominantly sensuous ; and this quality, modifying, and limiting by materializing, their religious and sentimental conceptions, made them in Art finite, and thence in sculpture and architecture, even more than in written poetry, classical ; that is, the forms, whether the human body, or a temple, or human life in a fable, definitely circumscribed the substance, which substance at the same time — owing to the overruling sensuousness of their minds — was not constrained by the form, but married itself happily thereto, the emotional and spiritual element in them not striving to burst the fleshly bonds, not stretching up yearnful toward the Infinite. Thence their sphere in Art was comparatively restricted ; and their great intellectual powers being concentrated upon a subject that presented itself round and compact and definite, the product — manipulated under guidance of their unfailing sense of beauty — was perfectly satisfying. Their nature was not commensurably developed on the upper side, as is proved by their greatest, that marvellous, creation, their mythology.

Now, Romantic or Christian Art is Art whose chief aim is, not to represent forms in their highest perfection, animated more or less with the life of the soul, but through the highest types of form to embody and give power to this life, all forms being used for and subordinated to a spiritual purpose, a means to incarnate the higher emotional. Thence, having a wider scope, Christian Art finds greater difficulty in harmonizing form and substance, and, though richer in opportunities and grander, and appealing to deeper sources in the human spirit, is more apt, through this very superiority, to fall short of the satisfying effect of Pagan Art.

Stand, not directly in front, but somewhat aside, where you have a view of one of the flanks as well as the front of a Greek Temple. From this one point the whole edifice is taken into the mind. Without stirring, you have in reach of your eye all its constituents: you imbibe at one draught its essence; you exhaust — no, that you do not, for "a thing of beauty," even the most bounded is inexhaustible, "a joy forever" — but you compass its whole nature. Within these two quadrangles is enclosed its entire circle of beauties, which are all external, for the interior is a confined dark receptacle, not to be trodden by the many.

Now look at a Gothic Cathedal from a similar point. The vision, and the thought behind it, are not at the first aspect rigidly pent into square frames, — the upper side whereof is in the Grecian Temple, bounded by the broad entablature with its multiplied layers of horizontal lines, — locking the building up in columned quadrangles; but the eye ranges upward unconfined, carried lightly by a crowd of lines, all tending skyward, which tendency, finding itself in the bulk of the building arrested by the limitations of human reach, and still unwilling to be balked, improvises, so to speak, the spire, wherewith it speeds on with disencumbered impulse until its point is lost in the blue above. Then, the eye redescending, cast it upon that file of pointed windows, deep and lofty, and upon that gigantic one, sun-shaped, a colossal front door-way for the sun, and beneath this, vast portals with festooned mouldings fringed with sculpture, through their deep narrowing recession inviting us inward. But before yielding to the invitation let us walk round the huge structure, light upshooting turrets and crocketed pinnacles and fantastic gargoyles and chiselled humanities, making the walk a continuous discovery, fresh aspects sprung upon us, shadows furrowing the ribbed surface, and the sun-rays playing through the tapering stories of the spire as though the transparence were a delight to them. We have passed through the door, and — when the first feeling of almost awe at the dim illuminated grandeur has somewhat subsided as advancing between stupendous winged colonnades of compound piers, wonders and beauties throng upon us — we perceive, that while to the eye and the mind the outside is the all in all of a Grecian Temple, in the Gothic Cathedral it is but the shell to the vast, variegated, living interior, — a canopy elaborate, ornate, radiant with symmetry, imposing with grandeur, but still in all its majestic pomp

10

secondary, a magnificent means for bringing about and empowering a deeper interior radiance and beauty and grandeur. "It is a house of garnered light, where rich, soft, iris-lustre is only a revelation to us of a glory before inherent in the common day, though invisible."[1] And as you silently move along its floor under the solemnizing spell of a religious majesty, the eye is acted on as is the ear when listening to a symphony of Beethoven, with its far glimpses, its boundless perspective of sound. While you are fascinated by figures in the foreground, appear behind them, successively issuing out of unfathomable recesses, stately shapes, harmoniously mingled to the sense though apart and contrasted.

The mastering charm of one of these vast, beautiful, mystically effulgent Cathedrals, (a charm unshared by the most perfect Grecian Temple,) is, that with its mazy heights, its distant lightly-poised roof, its lengthening shadowy reaches, vertical and horizontal, its mystic light, which has a dimness

1 *Art, Scenery, and Philosophy in Europe*, by Horace Binney Wallace.

The personal grief for the premature death of a gifted man is not necessarily deeper or longer than that for one unendowed for shedding light beyond a private circle; but scholars and thinkers will long grieve for themselves and for the public, that the author of the profound and beautiful thoughts and pictures contained in this fragmentary volume was lost so early to the world, to which the matured fruit of his pure and lofty genius would hardly have failed to be a governing light, an enjoyment deep and enduring.

even when most georgeous, it draws you towards the unknown. It symbolizes the infinite; it tempts you almost to measure with the eye the immeasurable; it seems about to reveal a glimpse of the unknowable; there is an awe, as though you stood on the verge of the sacred inmost circle where throbs the soul of things. With a startling vividness the spirit enjoys one of its high prerogatives; for to live ever consciously amid the unknown is a sublime privilege of man. Overarching him with incessant resistless attraction, the unknown becomes as integral a part of his life as his most familiar knowledge, his most transparent convictions. Working on him with expansive potency, stronger even than his experience, than the accumulations of what he knows, the unknown is his highest educator. His mind being boundless, is drawn into fructifying affinity with the Infinite, which calls forth the grandeurs of his being, as the darkness of night does the unspeakable glories of the sky.

This profound, mysterious, sublime element in our consciousness being, like all within or without us, beneficent in its purpose, is designed to be ultimately healthful in its action on the higher human life. But in undeveloped humanity the vague feelings it occasions are akin to those that come upon children in the dark, — feelings of fear and terror, whereof advantage has ever been taken, and continues to be taken, by the craft of self-worshipping priesthoods, to perpetuate the childhood of peoples and to keep men liable to outside power, delaying in them the age of manly maturity and individual moral self-dependence, — the age which must be attained ere men can possess full personal rectitude.

Doing the light but not unremunerative work of leisurely travellers, we spent over a fortnight at Dresden. Before quitting it I was to have another sight of the King.

At Moritzburg, seven or eight miles from Dresden, is a royal hunting-lodge, built in wilder times, and still resorted to for the princely pastime, the King betaking him thither for hunting the wild boar. Like spectatorship at the royal table, but not quite so accessible, this regal sport is hospitably opened to strangers. I sent a horse out the evening before, and the next morning drove to Moritzburg to breakfast. My brain became the ground for all kinds of huntsman's adventures. Boar-hunting might be dangerous: I was provided with a stout sword. I congratulated myself upon the so rare chance. Here, far away in the interior of Germany, a boar was to be hunted in a forest, and I was to be one of a royal party to the sport.

After breakfast I took a seat on the somewhat raised piazza of the inn. Just below me, in the open air, on a small table, was a breakfast, to which in a few moments sat down two young men. Their talk being loud enough to be heard much further than the piazza, I was obliged to overhear them, and to learn that they were Frenchmen,— the one *attaché* to the French Legation in Dresden, the other a student at Heidelberg. My thoughts being preëngaged, their lively talk — which was of themselves and other Frenchmen — was not to me so enlivening but that I longed for the hour to start. It came at last. Mounting, I rode a hundred yards or more along a high stone wall, somewhat beyond the corner of which I came upon the royal party, consisting of the King and his brother Anthony, with several of the household. They were just moving as I came up, in time to make the rear rider.

We soon entered a pine wood, and proceeding in silence, still keeping to the road at a moderate trot, we heard every now and then from a valley to the left the inspiriting cry of the dogs. Soon voices and steps came up behind me, and looking round I recognized the Frenchmen. The two talked so loud as to turn toward them the heads of several of the royal party; and dreading that I might be taken for a third, I separated myself from them as much as I could, riding to the side of the hindmost of the King's attendants, who seemed to be half groom half gentleman, but was probably wholly groom; for addressing him in German and putting on a deaf look as to the conversation behind us, in order that he might see that I was not of the French party, I got only a monosyllable in answer; and perceiving that he appeared as anxious to keep me behind him as I was to keep the Frenchmen behind me, I fell back — thinking to myself how I would dash ahead of him in the thick of the hunt — when a rattling volley of French drove me forward again. Presently a yell as of a hundred hounds swept up from the valley. The party quickened its speed. "Ah!" said I to the German, "the hunt, I suppose, is going to begin." — "Begin! It's ended, I believe." — "Ended!" — "Yes," said he with evident satisfaction, after listening for a moment, "they have caught the boar." — "Caught the boar! Who have caught the boar?" — "The huntsmen." The party turned to the left through another road in the direction whence came the cry of the hounds. We had now got into a gallop. Suddenly we halted. One of the attendants rode forward and soon returned. Upon this the King dismounted under the shade of some tall trees. We all followed his example. One of the Frenchmen was describing to the other a boar-hunt he had witnessed in France, (probably in a dream while asleep in a *quatrième* of the *rue Rivoli*,) and in so loud a tone that even the old King looked round. I drew off from them, fearing again that I should be implicated in their discourtesy. Presently I descried the boar, bleeding and exhausted, dragged along on his back by four men. They dragged him before the King. One of the attendants presented to his Majesty a drawn hunting-sword, and the King stepped up to the prostrate victim and pierced his heart. Drawing out the sword, he gave it back to the attendant, mounted his horse, and we, doing the same, trotted back behind him to Moritzburg. The wood through which we passed was intersected by smooth roads. The wall I had gone round on starting from the inn, was part of an inclosure in which are kept wild boars taken young in the forest. When the King wishes to have a hunt, a full-grown animal is caught in the pen, his tusks are sawed off, and he is then let loose.

In less than an hour we were back to the pen. I had gone out to hunt the wild boar in company with a King: I had witnessed a most unkingly hog-killing.

Two other feats which I performed, through royal and imperial assistance, were more successful, I having put on my head the hat of Peter the Great, and sat in the saddle of Napoleon, both of which are preserved in a collection of old arms and other curiosities. Nor should I fail to record, that one evening at the theatre I heard the Freyschutz, Weber himself leading the orchestra.

On the sixth of October, early in the morning, we left Dresden for Hertzberg, whence we started still earlier the next day, in order to reach Potsdam without borrowing more than an hour or two from the night. For the greater part of these two days our road lay through a sandy level covered with pines.

The sights of Potsdam are architectural, palace upon palace, the attestors at once of kingly pride and kingly littleness, and, I might add, of kingly presumption, — the builders, with an ambition as profane as futile, seeking, it would almost seem, to identify their coarse material handiwork with God's everlasting creation, by cumbering one of his warm, open-doored, bountiful palaces, the Earth, with their locked, luxurious, cold, petty, perishable and, for the most part, unsightly abodes, in their regal blindness not having the vision to perceive that man, whether king or subject, can only co-work enduringly with God through spiritual performance. Lord Bacon, to be sure, says, "buildings and foundations and monuments" are efforts toward that "whereunto man's nature doth most aspire, which is immortality or continuance." But then he adds, "the monuments of wit and learning are more durable than monuments of power or of hands. For have not the verses of Homer continued twenty-five hundred years, or more, without the loss of a syllable, or letter, during which time infinite palaces, temples, castles, cities have been decayed and demolished."

Frederick, called in English the Great, and in German the Unique or Only (*der einzige*), had an instinct to the same effect, for he attempted to write poems; and a printed quarto of these attempts is shown in one of his palaces, marked by the hand of Voltaire with numerous manuscript corrections, which are the attractive feature of the volume. To an intellectual sovereign, like Frederick, the more obvious path were through genuine, broad, home-looking statesmanship. I say more obvious, and not more easy; for it may be, that far-reaching, comprehensive, Christian, political insight is as rare as is poetical.

To call regal the blindness that misleads to superfluous masonry is unjust. It is human, and kings merely have in tempting profusion the material means to indulge the material desire. It is a blindness which comes of the self-will that insists on looking with the half — and with the lower half — of our mental optics. We persist in seeing but sensuously. Superfluous or superfine house-room or raiment or nurture, is like superabundant fat. Besides being cumbersome it is a sign of disease, and induces untimely death. Bodily needs and appetites are but the wheels that bear and carry forward the vehicle. Make them the vehicle, and you can carry only yourself, and that joltingly.

Self-seekers never find what they look for. The more they seek the less they find themselves; for such seeking is dog-like, with the nose to the ground, while the self, even in the sordid, is ever escaping upward, if not in acts or resolves, at least in repinings and longings.

I was in luck with inmates of palaces, having beheld at one deliberate sight five high royal personages, one a King in possession, and two of them Kings in prospective. Taking our stand (having attended the Catholic church at eight) a little after nine on Sunday morning the 10th of October, 1824, near the entrance to the church where the royal family go to worship, we had all to ourselves the regal party, consisting of the King of Prussia (he who was so smitten by Napoleon); the Crown-Prince, his eldest son; the Grand-Duke Nicholas of Russia, his son-in-law, with his Duchess, eldest daughter of the King; and the Princess Louisa, his youngest. The King was a tall, stout, awkward man, with a kindly expression. His son, the Crown-Prince, (elder brother of the present King,) was short and stout, his pug face of a pink hue, which in the latter years of his reign, through unremitted juicy nourishment, ripened to purple. The Grand-Duke Nicholas, who by his courage and energy made himself in the following year Emperor of Russia, was a noble body of a man, six feet two or three inches high, an imposing figure in carriage and countenance. He was one of those men whose will so energizes the faculties as to hang over them a reputation for intellectual superiority, a reputation which time is obliged to take down. Nicholas, with all the prestige of power still about him, judged while living by his latter contemporaries, was sentenced to be wanting as ruler in wise judgment. His Grand-Duchess was a fine-looking woman, worthy to walk beside such a figure. Her sister, the Princess Louisa, had a lively but not handsome face, and, although only seventeen, an oldish look. The young democrat noted that these royal personages moved their legs and arms just as other men do, and that they were even dressed like the well-clad crowd of ordinary immortals.

By half-past ten we were off from Potsdam, and reached Berlin in good time for the *table d'hôte* of the *Hotel de Rome* at two.

My uncle, as a proficient traveller, lost no hours; and so by four we had sallied into the Broadway of Berlin, the wide shaded avenue called *Unter den Linden*. The Diary notes "crowd of walkers: indifferent-looking population, and impossible to distinguish classes." We walked out through the Brandenburg gate into the Park, but were back in time to find ourselves seated at half-past five in the gilded, spacious Opera-hall to hear and see "The Vestal" by Spontini, the author himself leading the orchestra. Several boxes shone above their neighbors with the beauty of women; these, we found, were occupied by the families of Polish nobles. And so ended the Sunday, a variously busy day, begun with a church-service, and concluded, after the continental fashion, with the opera.

Historians should be optimists; the past should be accepted as good. Were one to say: for Germany, for Europe, it was a misfortune that Frederick (called the Great) inherited from his father a well-appointed army and full coffers, seeing that this inheritance tempted a capable, ambitious young King into the monstrous wrong of seizing Silesia, which seizure was the first act in a bloody drama of wars; such comment were a presumptuous censuring of Providence. And what work does the critic hereby lay on himself? Nothing less than the recasting of history! He might, in his impotent contumaciousness, carry sympathy with Brutus so far as to deplore the battle of Philippi, thus seeking to wrest from the Supreme guidance the procession of Roman events. And what will he do with them! He might go on to wish the Saracens victorious at Tours, or the action of Pontius Pilate stayed. Whoever should so misplace himself has no vocation to be an interpreter to his fellows, nor can he even draw due personal profit from the lessons recorded in the pages of the past. He but spins round on the pivot of a perverse wilfulness, soon to grow dizzy with the aimless whirl. The rivers and the rivulets of history, flowing from fountains and led by hands that lie utterly beyond human vision, even sudden, apparently irrelevant incidents, that to us look the play of very chance, may be the firm-set hooks whereon are hung long concatenations.

What we have to do with is Frederick as a fact; and the closer our judgment on him fits the actual man as God made him, the nearer we shall come to his historical import, and that of the many facts of which he was the centre. Beware of wishing him other than he was; for thus we entangle ourselves in a task fearfully above our strength. In the divine elaboration of European fates in the eighteenth century, had a human element like Alfred the Great been needed as successor to Frederick the flat-headed, an Alfred Prussia would have had instead of "Fritz" *the Unique*. Him we must submissively and even thankfully take as we find him. To find him just where he was we must look with clear eyes, eyes at once keen and visionary; and so looking, there will be no irreverent presumption, no barren wilfulness in detecting in the composition of Fritz an unwonted lack of the spiritual element. Mechanical and military was his mind, and his beliefs were material. Through the means of his rare military genius, his indomitable courage and will, he strengthened, we might say he furnished, the bones and muscles of a Kingdom, on his foundation built up to be among the primary Powers in Europe, with a progressive population, among whom the intellectual and spiritual make scope for their own culture, and who can now, from a high national German plane, forgive their pet King that he held their great-grandfathers hard in hand, that he could not recognize the broad German mother-tongue as a mighty instrument of Teutonic development, and scarcely knew that behind his body and his mind were spiritual potencies more precious than aught else in man, and so high, mighty, resistless and necessary, that they were regnant even over his unacknowledging self.

A wish to *re*-make history were shallow impiety; but we can make it. In the past we may not mingle, except as learners; but the present and future are a domain of which we can take partial possession, therein to work vigorously and potently to the moulding and coloring of events. Not in utter blindness, but with some selection of our point of *embouchure*, we flow as tributaries into the great channels of associated life. All living men are in a general sense makers of history, if they belong to a race deep enough to have a history; but there is a conscious premeditated action and influence which tell upon the inner currents that permeate a people, and this action and influence are strong and healthful according to the freedom and clear-sightedness of the predominant minds, and to the susceptibility of the masses to be the recipients and absorbents of the thought of the freer and wiser. For ourselves, whose democratic polity presupposes, for enduring success and progress, a larger and purer susceptibility of this kind than has ever yet existed, it behooves us thoughtfully to consider the political tendencies and prospects of our country, when we allow so many men who have reached no high stage of freedom to push themselves into high places.

The freedom here meant is moral freedom; and moral freedom depends on, consists in, active conformity to law. Law being as universal and beneficent as it is inexorable, pervades every thing, prevails everywhere. To go counter to law, is to shut out the sun that the eyes may do their function unsustained by his light, — which is, to put vision into bonds. To co-act with law, is to subordinate our thought and action to the invisible powers that work ceaselessly within and without us, — which is, to be so far free. He who should be in harmony with law always, in all provinces of life, bodily, mentally, morally, spiritually, would enjoy entire, absolute freedom. The crude, the immoral, the animal, the self-seeking, wear chains that circumscribe and obstruct them. The roving savage is as far from freedom as the coarse inebriate, or the refined epicurian of civilized Christendom; while Socrates and Washington enjoy so pure and wide a liberty as to be overflowing recipients and blessed dispensers of the divine illumination.

Berlin has none of the natural furtherances which a great city needs for a queenly preëminence and full prosperity. It has neither hills beneath and about it, nor a flowing river with depth and expanse of water, nor fertile fields around for the daily freshening of its markets. None of these has the Prussian metropolis, which lies in a barren, sandy plain, on a sluggish, petty stream. And yet it is now one of the foremost cities in Europe, having a population of more than half a million. The capital of a large kingdom, when once it gets to count from sixty to a hundred thousand souls, grows rapidly by the momentum given it by wide metropolitan privileges. Sovereign will first made Berlin a capital, and then regal wilfulness made it a capacious town. The arbitrary, indomitable Fritz, finding it too circumscribed for his ambition, enclosed a large outside area, and ordered his subjects to cover the enclosure with houses.

The gregariousness of the animal man, being a necessary antecedence to the earthly and superearthly progress of the immortal creature, he gathers himself into pens called cities, that he may the more readily be fed and shorn. To shape him into his proper proportions man needs to be compressed by men. Through the coöperative neighborhood, nay, the lively hostility of those he respects, his mind acquires symmetry and elasticity and compactness. For development of the multifold human faculties, collision and competition are indispensable. We rust unless we have others on whom, as Montaigne says, "to rub and file our brain," *pour frotter et limer notre cervelle contre celle d'aultrui.*

But dirt and disease come of this penning. The crowding together of heated multitudes engenders and aggravates vice. These close masses ferment. Not yet understood are the laws of association, whereby the grosser passional elements will be turned to clean productive forces, and hot humors that chafe and fester will have healthy outlets, and the warmest, strongest, most impulsive motions—motions that are now so often tyrannous, cruel, subversive—become creative, and the stronger for their loyalty, and be as chaste and salutary as solar influences on the planets.

Berlin, although six times the size of Dresden, has for the æsthetic traveller fewer attractions. In our nine days' tarry no good picture, or statue, or monument did we leave unenjoyed. We roamed the palaces, and sat in the theatres, and — what gave us unusual satisfaction, it being the first time that any of our party had visited such an institution — we spent a morning among the deaf and dumb, astonished and delighted at the success wherewith, in the education of their faculties, the humane and persevering ingenuity of art had been able to get round the irremovable obstructions of nature. The average number of the deaf and dumb in Germany, the principal informed us, is two to every ten thousand inhabitants, the proportion being greater in the north than in the south.

As the lecture-rooms of Goettingen reopened on Monday the 25th of October, we turned our backs upon Berlin on the nineteenth, and, repassing through Potsdam, — stopping only to eat a good dinner at "The Hermit," — arrived at ten at Wittenberg, to find the best hotel filled by the Duke of Cumberland and his suite. On issuing out of our inn the next morning before breakfast to glance round the old town, there, right before my uncle and me, in front, I think, of the very church on whose door Luther had affixed his momentous propositions, was a bronze statue of him. To my uncle it was not permitted to know Luther. He regarded him with that stolid, insatiable, Romish aversion, whose unutterability is deepened by the fear that mingles with the hate. If at any time the mighty shadow of the Giant crossed the disk of his sensations, it was only to be thrust angrily down into the nameless pit, to be there the compeer of Lucifer, chewing forever, beside that prime rebel, the bitter cud of bootless remorse for an impious revolt. But my uncle being preëminently an æsthetic traveller, caring little for history, or geology, or ethnography, or statistics, could look with critical calmness, with judicial impartiality, upon a statue even of the apostate Augustinian monk; and so looking, he pronounced it good. I did not seek to tread the learned halls that had been trodden by Hamlet. The search would have been vain, for a few years previously into that of Halle had been merged the renowned University, which has a passport to immortality signed by Shakespeare.

On leaving Wittemberg we diverged from the regular route to Brunswick, in order to make our night's resting-place at Koethen, where lived Hahnemann, whom my uncle wished to consult, and who just about that time had attained a European reputation. The eminent founder of Homœopathy happened to be absent, and to make up for lost way, we had to travel eighteen German miles, (about ninety English,) through Anhalt-Bernberg, Halberstadt, and Wolfenbuettel; so that, although we left Koethen at six on Thursday morning, it was three in the night when we entered Brunswick. Here we rested on Friday, and after another long day's pull got back to Goettingen on Saturday evening the 23d of October, 1824.

My next vacation was at Christmas, — a short one of two weeks, in which I made a trip to Hanover with Professor Saalfeld. Where and how was spent the long spring-vacation of 1825 may be read in the next chapter.

VIII.

Weimar.

DER Herr scheint unglücklich zu seyn: "the gentleman seems to be unhappy;" — said, in an audible whisper to her male companion in the public room of the *Erbprinz* in Weimar, a stout comely woman of five and thirty. Women are so charged with sympathy. In a tone half pleasant, half pitying she spoke, and made, I think, her words purposely audible to him who was the object of them; judging, perhaps, that knowledge of the proximity of interest would be a comfort. She judged rightly; for it was sheer loneliness that, from the bosom of a young man seated on the sofa, had brought up the sigh which awakened her curiosity and her good feeling.

Just a week previously, I had set out from Goettingen, in company with a Scotch fellow-student, Weir. My intelligent friend parted from me in Gotha, on a foot-excursion; and I, after spending two or three days at Gotha, in that state of half *ennui*, half restlessness, familiar to young men idling without acquaintance in a strange place, had, early on the morning of Sunday, the 27th of March,

1825, started alone, in a hired carriage, and, halting midway at Erfurt, to visit Luther's cell in the convent of the Augustines, had arrived at Weimar about noon; my purpose being to stop there a day or two, see Goethe if I could, and then go on to Leipsic and Dresden.

The feeling of loneliness which came over me on losing my companion, grew daily while I continued at Gotha, had been cultivated in the solitary drive of six hours, and now, in noiseless, secluded Weimar, with no social prospects to dispel its gloom, it reached a crisis in the sigh above-mentioned. The relief brought by this exhalation of heart-griping melancholy, seconded by the womanly comment thereon, was completed by the tickling fingers of the ridiculous, which, simultaneously with the arrival to my ears of the lady's words, were mirthfully thrust into my ribs.

To the fat lady I was grateful for her kindly succor; and, as a return, I determined to give her tender heart the solace of knowing that my "unhappiness" was not of a Wertherian hue. At the same time I wished to spare her delicacy the embarrassment of learning, from any too palpable act or movement, that I had overheard her remark. In a few moments, therefore, rising from my hypochondriacal position — viz., bent forward with elbows on knees, and face buried in hands — I discharged from my countenance all trace of dismal thoughts, and, walking springily across the room, smiled out of the window; so that her benignant eye could in a twinkle perceive that in my features there was no suicide.

After dinner (which at the public table of the *Erbprinz* was served at half-past one) learning that Goethe dined at two, I waited till a quarter past three, and then walked to his house in the *Frauenplatz*, (women's-place) not two hundred yards from the hotel. I had no letter, and knowing that Goethe refused to admit unlabelled visitors, I rang the bell with misgivings. The servant said, the *Herr Geheimerath* (the Privy Councilor) had not yet risen from table. "There," cried I vexedly to myself as I turned away, "by my impatience I have forfeited the at best doubtful chance of seeing the great man. The summons of his waiter from the dining-room to the door, he will feel as an intrusion on his privacy and comfort, and be thereby jarred into an inhospitable mood." I walked into the park, enlivened on a sunny Sunday afternoon with Weimar's quiet denizens. Towards four I was again ringing Goethe's bell. The servant asked my name. I gave him my card on which I had written, "aus Washington, America." My home being near the capital, of this I availed myself to couple my name with that of the sublime man — honored by all the hundred millions in Christendom — the presenting of which to the imagination of a great poet might, I hoped, kindle an emotion that would plead irresistibly in my behalf. The servant quickly returned and ushered me in. I ascended the celebrated wide, easy, Italian staircase. On the threshold I was about to pass, my eye fell pleasantly on the hospitable SALVE, inlaid in large mosaic letters. The door was opened before me by the servant, and there, in the centre of the room, tall, large, erect, majestic, Goethe stood, slightly borne forward by the intentness of his look, out of those large luminous eyes, fixed on the entrance.

In 1825, Americans were seldom seen so far inland. In his whole life Goethe had not probably met with six. The announcement of one for the unbusied moments of after-dinner, was I dare say, to the ever-fresh student and universal observer, a piquant novelty. His attitude and expression, as I entered, were those of an expectant naturalist, eagerly awaiting the transatlantic phenomenon.

Goethe was then in his seventy-sixth year; but neither on his face nor figure was there any detracting mark of age. Kindly and gracefully he received me; advancing as I entered, he bade me be seated on the sofa, and sat down beside me. In a few moments I was perfectly at ease.

At such an interview the opening conversation is inevitably predetermined. How long I had been in Europe; the route by which I had come; the sea-voyage. When he learned, that for fifteen months I had been a student at Goettingen, he inquired with interest for several of the professors, especially Blumenbach and Sartorius.

Opportunities of converse with the wise have ever been esteemed, by men eager for improvement, among the choice human privileges. Even now, when, through that far-reaching, silver-voiced speaking-trumpet — the printed page — the wise (and the unwise, too) can send their thoughts to the uttermost ends of the earth, personal contact with the gifted is still a gain and a rare enjoyment; for the most confidential writer cannot put all of himself into his books. In ancient times, when oral delivery was well-nigh the only means of communicating knowledge, men traversed seas to hold communion with philosophers and thinkers. What a position was mine then at that moment — seated beside one wiser than the wisest of the seven sages of Greece, in whose single head was more knowledge than in the heads of all the seven together; the wisest man then living, — nay, save two or three, the wisest that ever has lived. Across the Atlantic, through England and Belgium, over the Rhine (railroads and ocean-steamships were not in those days) I had come to be taught by the wise men of Goettingen. And here sat I, face to face with the teacher of these Goettingen teachers, with him from whom every one of them had learned, and from whom the best of them were still learning. Yet, in this interview with the chief of teachers, the wisest of the wise — an interview which hundreds of the highest men of to-day would almost give a finger to have had — in this privileged *tête-à-tête*, it was not Goethe who taught me, it was I who taught Goethe.

Reader, I take no offence at your contemptuous incredulity, but will briefly tell you how it was.

The news of the election of John Quincy Adams to be President of the United States had just reached Germany. Three days before, I had read it, while at Gotha, in a Frankfort newspaper. Goethe wished to understand the mode and forms of election. This I explained to him in full: the first process through electors, and then, as in this instance, the second by the House of Representatives. In stating that the people did not directly choose, but voted for a small number of electors, and that these then voted for one of the candidates, I used the word *gereinigt* (cleansed) to describe how the popular will, to reach its aim, was sifted through the electoral colleges. The term *gereinigt* pleased Goethe much. I used it because, being of one of the most federal of federal families, and not having yet begun to think for myself on political subjects, the breadth and grandeurs of democracy were still unrevealed to me; and it pleased Goethe because, broad and deep as was his sympathy with humanity, he was after all not omnisentient any more than omniscient. Thus had I the honor of adding a grain to the vast hoard of that omnifarious knowledge, which, passed through the bolting-cloths of a rich sensibility and bold imagination, furnished in abundance to his generation, and to all after generations, mental bread most nourishing and most palatable.

Thinking that a stranger, with not even the claim of an introductory note, should be content, after sharing with Goethe a brief fragment of his time, before a half hour had expired I rose and took my leave.

Back into the park I strolled, now no longer lonely: I was accompanied by the image of Goethe.

Goethe's face was oval, with grand harmonious lines, and features large and prominent, hair cut short, and gray without baldness, forehead high and roomy, largely developed throughout, and swelling in the upper corners, so as to unite in a fine curve the conspicuous organs of wonder and ideality. The whole head and face less massive than in the full-sized Paris engraving, which I have, after a portrait by Jageman; and also less broad than the engraving in Mrs. Austin's "Characteristics;" having the lightness and airiness which, in a countenance resplendent with mind, result from the harmony between the curve-inclosed breadth above and the strong basilar front.

At a German inn, especially in a small town, a stranger has resources which he will not find elsewhere in a public house. From their subdivisions, the Germans are a many-sided people. The Silesian and the Rhinelander, the Hanoverian and the Bavarian, the Viennese and the Berlinese — each of these is a different variety of the same species, the difference being perceptible in language, tone, culture. In Germany there is more culture than in any other country. Her high-schools, her universities, her libraries, are the best in the world, the most numerous and the most accessible. Nowhere is knowledge more valued; nowhere are there so many men with empty pockets and full heads; and nowhere has mere money less social weight. The German is, moreover, sociable; enjoying especially an after-meal talk. He excels, too, I think, in the rarest conversational talent — that of being a good listener.

From these causes, the company that at about eight (the supper hour) gathers in the public room, will be more various, more communicative, and more cultivated than at a similar meeting in France, England, or America. Our little party at the *Erbprinz* on Sunday evening, was a favorable specimen of such assemblages, and was as companionable as though we had been the assorted guests of a discriminating Amphytrion. Our chief talker was a young Lutheran ecclesiastic, who, voluble and well-informed, was carried forward by an inordinate momentum of animal spirits. Discussing the dress of the Protestant clergy, he averred that the cause of its being black was, that Luther happened to wear black. *Thaler* (dollar), he said, was derived from *Thal* (valley), the German silver coin of that denomination having been first made from metal mined in a valley of Bohemia. These samples of his learning I throw out as light exercises for antiquarians. Another of our company was an inspector of baths at Marienbad, who was modestly proud of some autograph verses given him by Goethe.

On Monday morning I awoke with such pleasant recollections of the preceding afternoon and evening, that I resolved to stop a day or two in Weimar — at least until time should begin to press idly upon me. Just before leaving Goettingen, I had received from a Boston friend and Harvard classmate a late number of the "North American Review," containing an article on Goethe's works. This I inclosed to Goethe with a note saying, that I took the liberty to send it, thinking that he might like to read what was written about him in the New World. The day I spent actively enough as sight-seer, seeing, among other things, the first printed Bible. Recollect that Weimar is Saxe-

Weimar, lying near to Erfurt; and that Eisenach, with Luther's watch-tower, the Wartburg, is part of its domain. Nowhere in Germany is the spirit of the mighty reformer more alive than among his Saxon kindred, the foremost in culture of the most cultivated people of Europe. It was fitting that to this central land should be drawn — as it was by the enlightened sympathy of a Saxon Prince — that mind which shares with Luther the intellectual sovereignty of Germany; and which, so unlike Luther's in its preponderances and in its *ensemble*, thoroughly harmonized with his in one deep characteristic; for Goethe was not behind even Luther in manly hatred of falsification and spiritual imposture.

Weimar, though a capital, being a small town, its sights were soon seen, and in the evening I was making inquiries about the routes to Leipsic, when there came a package from Goethe, containing the "Review" accompanied by a note of thanks, which stated that he had a few hours before received a copy of the same number from a friend in Berlin. But the pith of the note was in the end of it — an invitation to Goethe's house on the following evening.

Weimar being, as I said, a small town, and Goethe's house, even more than the palace, being its social centre, twenty-four hours were not needed to circulate through "society" the novel incident, that a young stranger, from far America, without letters, had, after an interview with Goethe, been invited to acquaintanceship with his family and circle. Of the mingled good-will and curiosity awakened by this distinction, I had evidence the next day. Early in the forenoon, Baron Seckindorf of Würtemberg, a fellow-student of Goettingen, whom, however, I had not known at the University, a modest, pleasing young man, called on me. He was spending his vacation with a cousin, the chamberlain of the Grand-Duke. We took a chatty walk together into the country. This visit was followed, after dinner, by one from three young Englishmen, acquaintances of Goethe's daughter-in-law, Frau von Goethe. At this time, and for several years afterwards (it may be so still), there were always young Englishmen temporarily resident in Weimar to learn German and mingle in the refined, easy society of the famous little capital, in which they were well received. By a progressive appointment of nature, strangers are ever warmly welcomed by women. For which, on the other hand, they are coldly eyed by the men.

Toward eight I repaired to Goethe's. In the large drawing-room, where he had received me on Sunday, were collected twelve or fifteen persons. But Goethe was not among them: he was unwell. Neither was his son present. Frau von Goethe, sprightly, intelligent, and graceful, did the honors with tact and cordiality. In five minutes I felt myself at home. Before the close of the evening it was determined that I should go to court — my new English friends taking on themselves to prepare me for the initiation. On the Continent, young Americans and young Englishmen readily fraternize.

My chief business, on the following morning, was to engage a waltzing-master. In the United States, during the first two decades of the present century, waltzing was not an essential of a gentleman's education. I had hardly been three days in Weimar when I found myself launched into the midst of its social stream. My brief journal — alas! too brief — sparkles with entries like these: "Wednesday: evening, at President Schwendler's; games. — Thursday: evening, at Frau von Spiegel's. — Friday: concert in the evening; Mozart's Requiem." But the great day was drawing near — the day of presentation at court.

In 1825 a European court held, in the imagination of a young American, a place beside images left there by the "Arabian Nights." It was a something gorgeous, glittering, remote, unapproachable; invested by history and poetry, and especially by romance, with elevation, splendor, and dignity. Kings, queens, dukes, lords, and ladies, were ideal, almost supermundane figures robed in Tyrian tissues; personages disinfected of all work-day commonness, impressive with practiced superiorities, their words commands, their looks glaring authority, their habits ever stately, their thoughts ever proud. The palace walls, shielded by a circumvallation of haughty ceremony, inclosed a precinct consecrated to jealous privilege. Into this charmed circle I was to enter. I was about to be an actor in an "Arabian Nights' Entertainment." I was about to read a chapter of history, in the first manuscript.

The awe which I felt on approaching such a crisis in my education, was somewhat allayed by daily social intercourse with the frequenters and constituents of the court. Especially did the talk of my English companions temper the effervescent spirit of imagination with the turbid water of reality. Still, it was not without trepidation that, at a quarter before three, on Sunday, April the 3d, in the year 1825, I descended the steps of the *Erbprinz* to enter the sedan which was to bear me to the palace. But before hiding me behind the curtains of the sedan, I must exhibit myself to the reader in court-dress.

Of the importance attached to costume at the courts of Europe, our whole country has lately[1] become aware, through the recommendation (which should have been positive instruction) sent by our government in 1853 to its diplomatic representatives. Thus, close upon the heels of the resolution

[1] This was first printed in 1856.

to go to court in Weimar, came the question of costume. A uniform of some kind, my English friends told me, I must have, the etiquette requiring it. I might follow my own taste and fancy in the color and style. One of these gentlemen — a man of parts and a graduate of Oxford, who had not even an ensign's commission — wore always at court the full dress of an English field-marshal, for which he had paid in London one hundred guineas. This ambitious fancy, by the way, cost him, a few weeks later, a ludicrous mortification; for the Duke of Clarence (afterwards William IV.) happening to visit the Weimar court, the young civilian, not wishing his field-marshalship to be challenged by so high a personage, withdrew for a week. Uniform I had none, and there was hardly time, had I even been so disposed, to have one first invented, and then made up by the tailor. The Englishmen cast about in vain to compound an outfit, by borrowing a coat from one, pantaloons from another, etc.; but among them were few superfluous articles of the courtly kind. At last I suggested, that with sword, chapeau-bras, knee-breeches, and silk stockings, I might possibly be admitted. The chamberlain was applied to. He received the proposal favorably, and would consider it. The matter was doubtless submitted to the Grand-Duke and Duchess. It is not at all improbable that even Goethe was consulted; for in Weimar, on any thing great or small, that was worth a consultation, his opinion was sure to be sought. Be that as it may, the chamberlain gave a consenting answer. Instantly a tailor was set to work on the "inexpressibles." One Englishman furnished a sword, another a *chapeau;* and so, with my black Stultz dress-coat, and a white vest, I was equipped.

A sedan is a light chair covered at top, with curtains on the sides and front, borne on poles by two men. An acceptable vehicle it is, where a pair of muscular human arms can be hired at the rate of twenty-five cents a day, where distances are not measured by miles, and when you are in full dress with thin shoes. It takes you in and puts you out under cover of hall or entry. A single servant in livery received me at the foot of the grand ducal stairway, and conducted me up into one of the receiving rooms, where were already several of my new native acquaintance. The company gathered rapidly, and we soon passed into a larger room, where I was presented to the Grand-Duchess. The Grand-Duke was ill. The Grand-Duchess was affable, and spoke of her son, Duke Bernhardt, who was then travelling in the United States. The introduction and conversation were as unceremonious as they would have been in the drawing-room of a well-bred lady in Boston or Baltimore. It was in this palace, at the head of the stairs I had ascended, that this Grand-Duchess received Napoleon the day after the battle of Jena, and by her calm courage, womanly dignity, and intellectual readiness, rebuked his vulgar violence, and extorted an unwilling respect. Ignoble natures, feeling nobleness to be a reproach to themselves, hate the true and pure, and, when unavoidably confronted with them, pay them a reluctant homage.

At three the Grand-Duchess led the way into the dining-room. About fifty persons sat down to a long table, the Grand-Duchess in the centre. Opposite and beside her were placed the elderly and officially elevated, while the younger members of the company mustered at the extremities, where, intermingled with the maids of honor, and remote from the stately regal centre, we were under no other restraint than that which refines the freedom of ladies and gentlemen. Behind each guest was a servant in livery. The dinner was princely. That it was, moreover, excellent, I have no doubt; but this I cannot affirm from personal judgment; for, happily, my critical craft in this significant province of civilized culture was only developed some years later. Of the service — at once lavish and refined — at the grand ducal table, take this as a sample. No sooner was a glass emptied than it was replenished by the watchful attendant. Through this silent savory sign your preference —

if you had one — was learnt, and hospitably indulged. You had, for instance, but to leave your Claret and Rhenish and Champagne unfinished, and to drain your Burgundy glass: so often as it was found empty it was refilled with Chambertin or Clos Vougeot, to the number of a dozen or more fillings, should any guest be rash enough to trust his head with so many. The dinner lasted till toward five, when the company followed the Duchess back into the receiving-rooms. Here we lingered less than a half hour, and then withdrew, to return at seven to tea, conversation, and cards. In the evening I left the palace early, having made an engagement to sup at eight with *Ober-medicinal-rath* (Upper medical Councillor) Froriep, a man of large knowledge and practical ability, and of distinguished liberality, and for these qualities much valued by the Grand-Duke.

The stranger is in luck who, on the same day, passes from the table of a sovereign to that of a burgher-subject. In the present case there was this beauty in the juxtaposition of the two tables, that the contrast between them was purely in the material and external. In the high essentials they were equal and alike, culture and intellect giving the tone at both. The guests of Mr. Froriep were four or five gentlemen, who, with his wife and daughter, made a party of about eight round his supper-table. Mr. Froriep's house was a modest centre of political liberalism. My fellow-guests were latent republicans. An open, legal, born, bodily republican could not but be an acceptable novelty. I sat down among them, a sudden welcome incarnation of their visions. The lively prose of conversation was occasionally pointed by written epigrammatic verse. One gentleman read some well-rhymed irony on the turning-lathe that had been set up at St. Helena in the room where Napoleon died. Another gave us a witty epigram on orders and ribbon-decorations.

On the following evening I had an opportunity of testing the obsequiousness of the bodily members to the mind's royalty, by straining to subject my femoral muscles to the desires of my cerebral nerves. There was a ball at Herr von Heldorf's. Never did dancer stand up with a more resolute will to dance. I had misgivings. Four or five lessons are a short apprenticeship to a new business. To legs thoroughly indoctrinated in the *pas de quatre*, the *pas de trois* is as steep up-hill work as the Kantean metaphysics to a Cartesian. Yet, to an unpracticed looker-on, the waltz seems so easy; and this deception through the eye is strengthened by the ear, which is captivated by the saltatory movement of the waltz-music. My utmost effort of will, the excitement of the scene and sound, and, more even than these, the indulgence and encouragement of my fair (and some of them were surpassingly fair) partners, could but partially and temporarily counterwork early thorough drilling and long habit. While my head and heart were intent on waltzing, my obstinate, undutiful legs would be thinking of the quadrille. I made lame work of it. Nevertheless, I staid until two o'clock, finding this the most instructive and the most delightful dancing-lesson I had ever had.

To the circle of the privileged, the doors of the palace were opened twice a week. Let me explain what I mean by "the privileged." At that time no Germans but such as had titles of nobility were *hoffähig*, that is, habitually admissible at the native courts. As much that they might adorn the court by their presence, as to do honor to their genius, were Goethe and Schiller ennobled. I never met at the palace one of the cultivated gentlemen with whom I had supped at Mr. Froriep's. Since that day, I believe, this feudal exclusiveness has been, in most capitals, extinguished or greatly relaxed, under pressure of the expansive spirit of these latter times. Once invited to the Sunday dinner at the palace, the invitation was repeated, as it was to other invited strangers, on every Sunday. But my English comrades had forgotten to put me through the form preliminary to an invitation to the Thursday evenings of the Grand-Duchess, on which evenings she had a reception or a ball. The omission I discovered, dining on Thursday at Herr von Schardt's. The preliminary form was, simply, to be presented to the Countess Schulemburg; and this, in order that I might not lose the Thursday of the following week, was done the next day.

From what has been related of the presentation to the Grand-Duchess, the logical reader will infer that one to her chief lady was not enveloped in many folds of formality. Opposite the palace is a large, plain building of three stories, similar outwardly and in inward structure to one of our college buildings at Cambridge or Princeton, called the *Prinzen Haus*, from having been once temporarily occupied by members of the reigning family. In the several stories of this edifice were lodged, in separate series of apartments, most of the ladies attached to the court. Here we were received by the Countess and her two daughters. I already knew the daughters, having half-waltzed with them a few evenings before. We were received, as at an ordinary morning call, without pre-arrangement, and without the other externals which, in a fashionable American house, are deemed indispensable — fine dressing and fine furniture. The toilets, sofas, tables, and chairs, were all of unobtrusive simplicity; nor was there in the demeanor of the inmates a trace of consciousness as to the character of these outward things. As ladies they received us, having no thought of their environment, and therefore not leading us to take thought thereof.

Nowhere in Weimar was there rich upholstery. Hundreds of houses in New York are more gorgeously furnished than was the ducal palace. It is true, neither Saxon princes nor Saxon nobles have much superfluous cash; but where there was any, it was likely to be invested in works of lasting beauty rather than in articles of superficial showiness, the obtrusive stare of which would discompose a gentleman, if any thing could discompose a gentleman. In Goethe's house the furniture was plain; but engravings, pictures, busts, spoke to the mind in his drawing-room.

It will be readily believed, that in this bright Weimar episode of my youth, there were no heavy hours. But had I been able to spend, without weariness, the whole of every day in dancing, gossiping, lounging, dining, supping, I should have been an unworthy participant of a society refined by the influence of Wieland, of Herder, of Schiller, and especially of Goethe, then the only survivor. It was vacation with me, and a salutary cessation of study; still two or three hours a day with the lighter kind of books, were as grateful a refreshment in the long holiday idleness as the whole holiday itself was to the working University term. I read for the first time Schiller's "Don Carlos," the glowing eloquence and aspiration of which make it so fascinating to the young, but which flinches somewhat before the calm gaze of mature criticism. Washington Irving and Fenimore Cooper were then in the bloom of their European reputation. From a circulating library I had "Tales of a Traveller" in the fresh, liberal, London edition, and a German translation of Cooper's "Pilot." A lady lent me a life of Iturbide, by himself. She did it on the ground that I was his countryman; for she said to me she was glad to meet an American, to make inquiries about a gentleman a friend of hers, and whom, as he was a distinguished man, she was sure I would know or know of. Where did he reside, I asked. In Mexico. The information I then gave, that my home was almost as far from the city of Mexico as from Weimar, seemed to confuse more than to satisfy or enlighten her. In 1825, Europe knew as little of the geography as of the politics of America. I am confident, that had my young English friends been closely questioned, it would have been discovered that some of them had not a perfectly distinct notion of the independence of the United States. The color of my skin was occasionally a surprise to inland Germans. One day, after dinner at the hotel, I vainly endeavored to make a Prussian understand how with us Church and State are separate. The most that I can hope is, that in his brain I planted a few grains of seed which, under later warmth, may have sprouted. On another occasion, I observed, at the public table, one of the guests, whose face I had not before seen, eying me with a look which denoted that, from some cause or other, my presence gave him pleasure. After dinner, when the company had thinned down to half-a-dozen conversable digesters, he said to me with a manner combining esteem with cordiality: "I am rejoiced to meet an American. You are a great people: you are the only people who are a match for the English. But for you, they would, by-and-by, through their naval supremacy, bemaster the world." An Englishman might have heard with more pride than offence the declaration, that only from her own loins could spring the race able to counterpoise England's preponderance over the globe.

The crop of hate which the English at that day reaped from the seed of arrogance and contempt, sowed broadcast, as they journeyed through the countries of the Continent, has since been largely supplanted by a growth of international knowledge, bearing the healthful fruit of mutual respect and leniency. How pert a mischief-maker is ignorance. Of what reciprocally the feelings then were between the islanders and the dwellers on the main, I had an amusing exemplification. On a forenoon, one of the Englishmen called for me to take a walk. "What's all this fuss about — who are these epauletted fellows on the stairway?" he asked, as he entered my room. "The Elector of Hesse Cassel arrived half an hour since," I answered; "he is about going to the palace, and these are his suite, waiting to attend him." This Englishman was a type of the animal, muscular, coarser John Bull. He was above the middle height, squarely built, broad across the shoulders, with good, regular, not prominent features, a short face and round head, a steady blue eye, and tanned skin. Lining the somewhat broad stairway, from the upper landing to the bottom, were ranged six or seven officers of rank, in full glittering military dress, forming a double row for their master to pass through. The Englishman, as he left my door, struck his hat down on his head, giving it a saucy cant on one side, thrust his hands into his pockets, descended the steps with a careless, loose gait, cast his eyes neither to the right nor to the left, utterly ignoring the presence of the dazzling Hessians, and whistled as he went. I, who had stopped a moment to turn the key, being several paces behind him, had a full view of his proceeding and its effect. Contempt could not have been more emphatically expressed, even in words. And yet, to no one of the contemned was it directly conveyed; for his eyes took no note of them. With motionless wrath, the Hessians beheld this sudden insolent apparition. Their mustachios seemed almost to curl with impotent rage; for the offence was hardly a tangible one; moreover, it was committed by an Englishman — a most palpable Englishman. The Hessians were, doubtless, brave men, and bore no especial love to Englishmen; nevertheless, they would, probably, on the spot, have resented the act, indirect though it was, had it been committed by a man of any other nation. No other European would or could have done such a thing. No other, however brave, would have had the boldness and independence to give his scorn such expression. The habitual consciousness of freedom — a consciousness which no other European had then, or (alas!) has now — gave to the Englishman a virile tone, which enabled him to do what none other would dare do; and, more than this, to do what was offensive, and almost indecent, with impunity; for these very Hessians, not one of whom could even have felt moved to such a deed, and who were boiling with constrained anger, were yet unconsciously and unwillingly awed into passiveness by the manly inward power which enabled the Englishman to do it.

On the following Sunday I was presented to the Grand-Duke. Carl August was below the middle height, with a large, square head, and well-composed face, expressive of intellect and energy. From recent illness, he was still pale and feeble;

and being hard of hearing, in the interview before dinner, I had to raise my voice, which seemed to annoy him. I was glad when our brief conversation ended, and I thought his Highness somewhat grumpy. Now, among my precious memories is this: that in his own palace, I was presented to the enlightened, hospitable prince, the pupil of Wieland, the generous protector of Schiller, and the life-long fraternal friend of Goethe.

And have you nothing more to say of Goethe? some of my readers may here ask. Would that I had. But, to be frank, I thought very little about Goethe. If self-reproaches were, in such a case, of any avail, briskly would I join the reader in heaping a mountain of them on my own head. Here was, indeed, a gigantic example of the wasted opportunities of youth. True, with the most intense will, I could not have had another interview with Goethe. From the illness into which he fell, two days after my arrival, he did not recover until I had left Weimar. His daughter-in-law promised me that I should see him again; but the day never came. I spent, however, three weeks, lodged within a stone's throw of his house, in the town where he had lived for fifty years, and where there were scores of men and women who had witnessed his arrival, and a whole population familiar with his person and his every-day life. I might have questioned the recollections of octogenarians, the experience of the middle-aged. I might have sought out his old servants, his old enemies, and his old and his new friends — he had no new enemies. I might have tracked him to Ilmenau and to Jena. Now, presupposing the miracle, that a young man of twenty-two could have so appreciated Goethe — have so seized the significance of his deep life — have so mastered the import of such a career, as to have originated the inquiry, and then pursued it with a sagacious zeal; still, although many particulars might have been gleaned, whose valuable meaning sympathy would interpret, the result would probably have been far less affluent than you hope. Those among whom he lived did not fully realize his greatness. Familiarity with a great man does not breed indifference; but there may be even respect and affection without the key of sympathy, which alone can unlock the treasury of a mind. On his neighbors and fellow-townsmen the impression of any great man is stamped more by the acts and qualities wherein he is like themselves, than by those which constitute his greatness. Besides, in the many — without regard to class — there is a special obtuseness to the claims of poetic power — an unwillingness to acknowledge, grounded on an incapacity to perceive, the superiority of the creative nature. An extreme instance of this dulness I witnessed in England, a few years ago. While I was at Malvern, Wordsworth (it was only a year or two before he died) arrived at the house of a relative, on the opposite side of the Malvern Hills. Wishing to shake hands once more with the great poet, I hired a donkey-carriage, to drive the two or three miles round. Had I taken the shorter foot-path, over the hills, I should have met Wordsworth, who, then in his eightieth year, crossed them that very morning, on foot. The driver — whom we had often before employed — was a middle-aged man, intelligent and thriving. As we drew near, I told him we were going to see the poet Wordsworth, the greatest man then living in England. The house stood at some distance from the public road, and the driver getting down to open the gate that led to it, I said he need go no further with the carriage — we would walk to the house; and then, bethinking me, I added, "but perhaps you would like to take the chance of seeing Mr. Wordsworth; in that case we will drive to the door." "Oh! no, sir," he answered, "I don't know what good that will do me." I should have rejoined, "drive in, at any rate, perhaps the donkey will like to see him."

To return to Weimar.

One afternoon we found ourselves — two or three of my English fellow-idlers and myself — in the drawing-room of Madame Goethe. Goethe's son and daughter-in-law had in his house up-stairs, a separate suite of rooms. The Englishmen —

more muscular than mental — soon got into a romp with several young ladies, who happened to be present. Not being so demonstrative, I was a tranquil, and by no means admiring spectator of the hoydenish flirtation. German houses are not the most solid. The room so shook, that I feared some cups, on an *etagère*, would leap to the floor. I said to Madame Goethe, "Will not this disturb your father-in-law?" "Oh! no," she answered, "he will not hear it, and if he does, he will not mind it." This is another precious, and, I may add, unique memory, that, in Goethe's own house, I once raised my voice, to protect his sick nerves from the possibility of a shock.

On the last Thursday of my stay, there was a ball at the palace. I was not yet qualified to take a master's degree in that department of knowledge which now, throughout all Christendom, is in ball-rooms the most profitable. In the art of waltzing, I was still a learner. But, in amends, I was so proficient in the less passionate and more variegated, the gentlemanly quadrille (in my dancing days we called it cotillon,) that mortification at failures in the native dance was counterbalanced by triumphs in the foreign; and as things from abroad are, for their very rarity, esteemed more than their equivalents of home-production, I gained, on the Weimar floor, by my skill in the French step, far more credit than I lost by my rawness in the German. In truth, at that day I had the French step, in all its elaborate diversity, completely at my toes' ends. Here let me gratefully pause, to pay tribute to the two professors of this elegant art, to whom I owed my mastership, and its consequent honors. Doubtless there are still living, in the District of Columbia, some young grandfathers, and younger grandmothers, who can in memory go down into the first decade of the present century, and draw up thence cheerful images of their embryo selves, when, with their heads not much above the level of his knee, they were ranged in line by the fiddle-bow of Mr. Generee. This gentleman was a sample of the French dancing-master of that age — courteous, patient, straight, graceful, with a calf like the Borghese gladiator. My legs were very, very short, when they did their then utmost to mimic the motions of his, in Washington, and also in Bladensburg; for (alas, the decadence of ancient respectabilities!) the village of Bladensburg (not yet historical) could then muster a dancing-class large enough to draw the professor five miles out from the capital. What, under the tillage of Mr. Generee, could, with such tender sap, shoot only into promising buds, bloomed out, a few years later, into a luxuriant crop of steps, under the culture of Mr. Guillou of Philadelphia, a gentleman who must be the object of pleasant recollections to hundreds of still breathing pupils, and who, moreover, for his intrinsic worthiness, was by a large circle beloved and esteemed. Since those modest days, the amorous waltz has, in America, too, so thrust the quadrille aside, that the present generation of dancers have no experience of the French expertness of their predecessors. Will it be believed, that for the *chassez* forward, I had four different steps, with *balancez* to match? Then, we did not walk through the figures, we danced conscientiously from beginning to end; and, under inspiring influences, displayed our whole variegated store of movements. This I did not do in the private houses, even of Weimar. But in the palace, and my last ball, and goaded by the easy superiorities of gyrating competitors, I performed my part in a style which would have rejoiced the muscles of my old teachers, who I can, if I please, now have the satisfaction of believing were (according to recent theories of trans-terrestrial existence) happy witnesses of that hour's triumphs, hovering above me, their incorporeal legs following the Grand-ducal music, in a duet of silent, invisible, saltatory delight.

The cautious, sensitive, and calculating, advise that an incident which, however true, yet so outstrips the common march of events as to be difficult of belief, should not be chronicled, lest thereby the credibility of the writer be brought into question, and not only the exceptional fact itself be rejected, but discredit be thrown on all the other statements of the narrator. Such suppression I hold to be unworthy a manly mind. Of the consequences of telling the truth, conscious rectitude should be utterly thoughtless. What is true, keeps true, despite disbelievers; and on them alone falls the penalty of ignorant disbelief. Should readers doubt the fact I am about to relate, I shall be sorry — on their account, not in the least on my own. While the younger company were dancing in the ball-room of the palace, the Grand-Duchess, with some of the elder nobles, spent the evening in muscular sobriety, at whist, in another room. Recollect that this sovereign Grand-Duchess was she who successfully rebuked Napoleon. Now for the incident. At courts, there are always courtiers watchful to minister to the pleasure of their sovereign. The Grand-Duchess — informed, doubtless, by these — temporarily left her cards and walked into the ball-room to see the young American dance a quadrille! This I only learnt at the end of the dance, as her Royal Highness was returning to the card-table. Had I, when on the floor, been conscious of so august a spectator, I cannot now say but that the effect would have been depressing, instead of elevating. Whether the Grand-Duchess left the card-table at the end of a rubber, or at the end of a game, or at the end of a deal; or whether she had just been a loser, and was therefore glad of any excuse to break off for a while, in order to change the luck — this it was impossible for me to inquire into, however valuable knowledge of such concomitants would have been, as indicating more definitely the animus of her extraordinary act.

And now, the vacation was drawing to a close. I had but a few days more in Weimar. On Friday, the day after the grand ball at the palace, there was, in the evening, a party at the rooms of the Countess Julie von Eglofstein, then about thirty, one of the unmarried ladies of the court, distinguished, in Germany, for accomplishments, taste, culture, and a rare Juno-like beauty. Here I saw for the first and only time — and that but for the brief moments between the rising and the falling of the curtain on a *tableau vivant*, in which he was the leading figure — the dark, large, Italian features of Goethe's son. On Saturday, I left cards, P. P. C. On Sunday, I dined for the last time at court. Of this dinner, I have, too, a pleasant memory. I had failed to get the seat I aimed at, beside the Countess Eglofstein. On one side of her was a stranger to me; on the other, a young Englishman, whom I knew but slightly. Before the company had got quite settled in their places, I made a supplicatory appeal to his generosity to exchange seats with me — he, I said, was to be months longer in Weimar, it was my last day. He rose and gave me his seat. He did it with a kind and ready courtesy which became one of his lineage. His name was Shelley, and he was related to the illustrious poet.

On Monday, the eighteenth of April, I was on my way to Goettingen, one of the fifteen hundred students who, making travellers' lines from all points of the compass, turned their faces back toward that learned centre, where, in a quiet little Hanoverian town, was then the foremost university of Christendom.

And so ends the record of Weimar, the reading of which will, I trust, afford some fraction of the gratification derived from the recording. A subtle pleasure there is, more sweet than sad, in thus minutely reviving the festal days of the far-off past, when life moved without burdens, and was too happy to think of its happiness. Like blossoming flowers, seen in a window through the fast-falling snow, are these pictures of youth, beheld through the chill of our autumn and winter years. Strange and warm they look, and so distant. In their freshness and unfading smile, they stand apart; and yet, they are parcel of our present life, which they temper, mingling in it like the soft tongues of childhood in the hard converse of age.

IX.

FROM GOETTINGEN TO ANTWERP.

ANOTHER semester at Goettingen would have been a tedium. I had exhausted the University. What! the hundred professors, could they teach you nothing more? The professors had an undiminished capacity to teach, but my capacity to learn was much reduced. From a cask of the best wine you can only pour into a bottle a fixed measure. Was I then already full? This illustration is defective, for a bottle has no expansibility; whereas the living brain is indefinitely capacious, and, drawing life from what it imbibes, the more it takes in the more it thirsts. But what is taken in must be assimilable; and even then there needs timeliness in the taking.

Had I been of a merely receptive nature, I might have spent years at Goettingen in diligent accumulation, adding to my learned stores with each recurrent solstice, resting and refreshing myself by change of intellectual diet as I passed from one "Faculty" of the bountiful University to another. But—unconsciously then to myself—knowledge was to me but a means of culture.

Acquirement and study and the thoughts of others are but instruments for unfolding and ripening my own powers. Had there been in the "Faculty of Philosophy" a genial literary department, so that, having now mastered the language, I could have enjoyed high lessons in criticism, in the principles and mysteries of style, in poetry, a new life would have been given to a fourth semester. But there was nothing of the sort. Bouterweck's was the only course on Literature and Æsthetics; and his was a mind without insight or original reach. Mueller's "Archæology" was more learned and historical than æsthetical, and thence, although instructive, did not take tight hold of the feelings and reason. In the finer literary province, teachers whose lessons would have awakened creative aspiration, who could have met and embraced the inner deeper wants, were not to be had in Goettingen. And where are such to be had?

I had followed most of the courses on subjects of general interest, subjects a scholastic introduction to which contributes to give the necessary breadth to the foundations of a liberal education. Had not an introduction such as was secured by one course of lectures been all-sufficient for the profit then attainable, I might have resorted to the *auditorium* of Sartorius to learn wherein his teachings in Politics and Political Economy differed from those of his rival, Saalfeld. The difference I should have found to be neither deep nor broad; for the treatment of politics in German universities was then (and probably is still) more mechanical and formal than vital; and as to Political Economy, I had had already too much of the husks that are passed off for succulent grain, having at Harvard gone studiously through the treatise of the elder Say, — at that time the text-book there, — and having just taken copious notes under the desk of Saalfeld.

To me it seems that Political Economy is very much overrated. It is referred to as if there lay within its precepts some golden key that could unlock the largest social problems; as if one who should have mastered its mysteries were master of a secret that was to lighten all public burdens. Now in it there are neither mysteries nor depths. Its substance is as external and subservient as are its forms and methods. In the vast circle of agencies that affect human association, Political Economy stands as secondary to all the controlling powers as Chemistry does to vital force. Chemistry has to do with dead elements, or matter unorganized. Wealth and material products, wherewith Political Economy has to do, are the results of action and influences involving considerations and principles that lie above its range. Like Chemistry, Political Economy can merely analyze; and it is only lifeless elements that can be analyzed. But society is a never-ending synthesis,

The importance bestowed on the body of rules and forms and judgments that have been deduced from observation of the action of government on the production, distribution, and consumption of material products, to which is given the imposing name of Political Economy, is due to the material tendencies of the past century. People thought that by systematizing an accumulation of empirical results into regulations for the management of the material resources of a nation, they had found a political philosopher's stone. Beginning at the wrong end, they sought to lift effects and secondary antecedents into causes, striving to make that primary which is altogether dependent. What vitiates the whole procedure, taking all life out of Political Economy, is, that to control the production (to say nothing of the distribution and consumption) of wealth you must control the whole producer. You cannot separate the worker from the man. It is this disjunction of him, as though he could be dualized, this mechanizing of man, that makes the whole pretended science of comparatively little account. Of human work Political Economy relates to but a part, and that the grosser part, and is thence not only deficient, but deficient there where play the highest forces of human vitality, and is chargeable with attempting, through an inferior province of human interests, to control the nobler. Its more confident votaries remind me of a man who many years ago came to me in Baltimore to enlist my editorial interest in establishing Lyceums; not because they were good things as making occasions of bringing people together for intellectual culture, but because, as he earnestly insisted, they would be the means of universally enlightening the population, and thence of rapidly reforming all moral evils and abuses. A mechanical contrivance was to regenerate the world!

Humanity at this moment urgently needs, not to know what under existing institutions is the best way for government to interfere with the labor of individuals, but how to bring order into that labor itself. Human work, not only the father of all material wealth, (Nature being the mother,) but designed to be the agent of all human good, moral, intellectual, material, cries for organization, in order that its mighty function be duly performed. To still the discords of civilization, work must be organized. And the organization of work demands a reach of thought with the coöperation of sympathies that make a minor section in the mental outlay of a thorough-paced political economist. Hence, the profound all-embracing social questions that have begun to agitate Christendom are met with repugnance or contempt by this class of writers, who, being mostly men wanting in geniality and juiciness, exhibit much of that quiet self-sufficiency to which those are especially liable who, incapable of seizing the whole of a subject, fasten voraciously on that lower side of it which is within their grasp.

Much more had I found in Goettingen than I came thither to seek. Through the lecture-rooms I had sought admission into the wide populous precincts of history and politics and public law, and statistics and æsthetics and natural history, to found, through introduction by those who had a cordial familiarity with these intellectual potencies, acquaintanceship that might in after years ripen to intimacy. But I gained, besides, what was still better worth the labor expended, namely, an introduction to the spirit and method, the thoroughness of German mental work. I learned to know (with all the possible profit consequent on such knowledge) the wise impartiality, the manly search for truth, the thoughtful grasp wherewith the scholars of Germany handle the great themes of science and study. And further, I brought away a treasure, the full value whereof I could only learn much later — the German tongue. What seemed then but a means of opening my ears to the oral knowledge of the lecture-rooms, was to be that of silently laying bare to me the thought and beauty and wisdom that lie within the pages of Lessing, and Schiller, and Richter, and Goethe.

The gentleman who, at the suggestion of a prime minister, studied Spanish in order to obtain the secretaryship of the mission to Spain, and who was told — to comfort him for the disappointment of not getting it — that his toil had not been in vain, as he would now have the happiness of reading "Don Quixote" in the original, had a minor indemnification to that of him who, by mastering German, has earned a life-estate in the wealth of Goethe. Goethe was one of the most richly-endowed of the sons of men, many-sided and broad-sided and bright-sided. Having the supreme gift of imaginative transfiguration, he gives to truth winged bodies of beauty, wherewith to hover over and attract, and delight while instructing, the more capable of his fellows; he having first, through this high power of imagination, gained insights that purged his nature and his knowledge, and gave a symmetry to his thought while it stimulated its vast fertility. Goethe's thought is not for Germans only but for men. His wisdom is a clear distilment out of the profundities and brilliancies, the manifold capabilities and yearnings and achievements of humanity, which in him flower with a beauty and fullness whereof we have in Shakespeare alone a richer example. So much breadth with so much subtlety, so much largeness with fineness of texture, so much power with the most delicate literary susceptibility, are nowhere else to be met with. He took up into his mind from without more than other men, because his capacity of appropriation was so wide and at the same time so minute; and through all the months and weeks and days of eighty years his thought was fed by his sensibilities with fresh food, so firm and healthy was his organization. Through sympathy for all that lives, he joyed in multifarious observation and study, and in a lifelong productiveness; and through love of the beautiful and the true, he sought ever a better than we have to-day, asking with his latest breath for "more light."

Thus had Goettingen sown on my mind good and various seed, and much of it — as much as I could bear. To have stayed longer would have crowded the soil and have been more harmful than helpful. But I could not have stayed longer. Even a month more would have been as distasteful to me as to the palate of a healthful diner were the piling of food into his stomach after a full repast. Of the German food which at that stage of mental growth I was capable of digesting, I had my fill. What was best for me I could not then definitely *know*, but I *felt* it with something higher than an instinct.

And so, having taken leave of kind friends, — some of them fellow-students, at the steps of the *Eilwagen*, — at midnight on the twenty-fourth of September, 1825, I bade adieu to Goettingen with sorrow and joy, — sorrow at breaking the many ties which affection spins out of hale hearts, and with the joy which is the buoyant child of hope when the young start on a new journey in life, untrodden paths beckoning them with promises and fascinations. As companion to Cassel I had my former fellow-traveller, Weir. At Cassel the next day we dined with a friend of his, Mr. Schiebe, who held a minor post under the Hessian Government, and who dispensed to us a modest cheerful hospitality.

Weir was a manly Scotsman, whose way through the brambles and tangles of the world was to be cut by himself; he had a head-piece well equipped for the work. Like most of his young countrymen at Goettingen, he had been there for the sake of Civil Law; but, with the aspiration for which at that time were creditably notable other of his fellow-lawyers at Edinburgh, he was drawn into the freer fields of literature, and had already made his entrance into print, through that open, inviting, and almost unavoidable modern door, the public journals. He was of a temper at once joyful and earnest. He and Dwight had one evening a lively encounter as to the superior prowess of the Scot or the Yankee in pecuniary keenness and the arts of thrift. Dwight's stories were rather the most stringent, when Weir, to overwhelm him with one concentric blow, declared that in Scotland they have a saying, that it takes two Jews to make one Scotchman. "But we," rejoined Dwight, "have a saying, that it takes two Scotchmen to make one

Connecticut-man." Weir spoke with modest pride of friendly acquaintance with Sir James Mackintosh; and it was probably the influence of Sir James that led him later in life to London, where he died in 1858, having been for several years the efficient editor of the leading liberal English journal, the *Daily News*.

Part of the journey to Frankfort was more than beguiled by the talk of a Professor in the Giessen *Gymnasium*, or College — one of that large class of devoted indoor workers who keep the scholarship of Germany up to so high a level. At Frankfort I fell in again with Watson, — a meeting as agreeable as it was unexpected. Watson, somewhat past the university-age — being about twenty-six — was one of several Englishmen, who, during my stay at Goettingen, had at different times spent a few weeks there, attracted by the renown of the University, then preëminent in Europe, from its uniquely brilliant band of teachers, the German accessibility of its rich museums and botanical gardens, its observatory, and its vast teeming library, with doors wide open to all comers. In that land of intellectual husbandry many are the men who spend years in a university-town, whither they had been drawn as studious visitors, getting firmly domesticated among the ready instruments and facilities for acquirement and culture. Several were pointed out to me who, having come to Goettingen to pass a few months, found themselves mentally in so warm a nook that they had there nested themselves for life.

One whose first love dies unenjoyed hugs the remembrance of a hope, which, fed by tenderest imaginations, becomes a delicate possession of the heart, growing even more exquisite with years. The mind, under the sad sweet pressure, exerts its preservative and at the same time its creative power, beautifying while it perpetuates. With feebler grasp, but with kindred fruition, the memory fondles with affectionate fancies friends of early days whom death has taken ere the impulsions of youth have stiffened into self-seekings, and suspiciousness has encroached on frankness, and the practices and collisions of over-busy overbearing life have hardened the moral texture, transfiguring early companions.

Watson was a friend and pupil of Coleridge. One day he took from his trunk a volume of "The Friend," and read a sentence *apropos* to our talk. The words went little further than my outward ear; for Coleridge was then to me but a shimmering name. Only several years later was unsealed to me the page whose splendors and profundities were to be a resource even in maturest years. That one sentence may, however, have been a seed; for through "The Friend" (in Marsh's American edition of 1831), it was that I first made acquaintance with Coleridge, and took him into my heart, to be there a life-long warmth and illumination.

Of a nature to love one whom he so much admired, Watson, though not of the calibre to be an interpreting constructive disciple, was probably a cherished pupil of the kindly master. Tall and well built, of a nervous rather than muscular structure, he had a fine head thickly topped with strong, half-curly, black hair, and a countenance, in shape and feature Roman, uniting sweetness with intelligence, on which when he laughed, as he did often, a glittering row of teeth threw a light partly physical, partly moral, flashing on you the purity and probity of the man. Over his circle his early death must have shed more than the common family gloom. He was one for affection to twine around and for hope to build on.

What a regenerative fecundity in Nature, that she keeps her bloom undimmed against the hourly fading of so many blossoms and flush flowers. In other ranges than the supreme human still more lavish of life is she. Go into the summer fields, crushing as you step myriads of new-born creatures; gather in spring from your trees, for their protection, a basket of cocoons to burn their countless germs; tread in some watery inland nook among the spawn of salmon; think of the hourly devastation through earth and ocean by animals that feed on their living subordinates. Nature is a vast throbbing *vivarium*. Life, multitudinous, elastic, unquenchable, defies loss or lesion, and renews itself as the sun his heat. Death is in every case but a transformation. Nothing dies. Through the Oriental belief in the transmigration of souls glimmers a divine truth. All apparent death is but a transmigration of life into another form — a renewal through change. The imperishable Protean vitality shifts its embodiment. When in our more carnal and timid moods we consider human pain and destruction, through disease and war and many-legged misery, we moan and doubt, and in thought almost blaspheming, are ready to impugn Providence. But moans and doubts are but the writhings of our frailty; and law, seemingly heartless but really merciful, plies ceaselessly through daily death; and we, as we quicken with spiritual growth, recognize its beneficence.

Having come in a packet-boat from Frankfort to Mayence, we loitered down the Rhine on foot, betaking us, when tired, to a skiff to float with the current of the old river, then innocent of steam. The vines were at their flood of spicy juice, ready to overrun into the wine-tubs. Already the autumn sun threw, even with his noon-day fire, rock and slope and ruin into the tender relief of long shadows; the landscape lying still and silent that the celestial artist might the more effectively lay on his many-tinted strokes; or, soft breezes at times making a tremulous interlacing of leaf and light. But young blood is too ebullient for full reflection of the calm beauties and grandeurs of Nature, her tranquil images being made to quiver in the headlong current. Youth's business is to absorb, not to reverberate. Intellectual pleasures are heightened, nay, almost in many cases created, by the consciousness which comes and deepens with years. Indeed, the broader the life and the more cultivated, the greater should be the zest of all one's joys, even the lower. In old age life should still have its daily freshness and newness. The source of youthful enjoyment is growth, and growth should never cease. The stars lose not their sparkle with years; and the soul has within it a fire to send with every new day a new flame into the eyes and thoughts. But in our later earthly years the soul gets smothered by misgrowths and bedraggled memories of the senses, and its light darkened by opaque or intrusive or impossible desires. The body, to keep its health, throws off daily the effete, what to the tissues has become barren, its *scoriæ* and recrement; and the mind, for its cleanliness and sprightliness, should not seek to live in manhood on the dross of youth, or paralyze itself in age with trying to find nourishment in what should be the sediment of manhood. Old age may be as hopeful, as freshly fed with imaginations, as blithe and secure as youth, if on its way it shall have purged itself of untimely obsessions, if it will not let the soul — soon to slip its hold on earthly hooks — be besieged by earthy desires or bewildered by material fancies, nor the sacred chambers of the heart be haunted by the phantoms of passion.

We parted, my friend and I, at Cologne, and, by the old road through Aix-la-Chapelle and Liege, the heavy, steady, drowsy *diligence* carried me again to Antwerp.

The fruit I had gathered in Goettingen found no market in Antwerp. None that I came in contact with valued me for having in my absence of twenty months acquired a right of property in *Faust* and *Wilhelm Meister*. There the jewels, wherewith the creator of these masterpieces has perennially irradiated the brow of humanity, were no more distinguishable than in a dark chamber would be diamonds from garnets. A community purely Catholic offers small scope for the spiritualities of literature. The freedom of intellectual play enjoyed on these heights endangers priestly predominance.

A people who has not produced good lasting books continues, in spiritual nonage, a nation of pupils — what Rome likes and fosters. And yet, from that whereof literature is made the papacy has drawn much of its power and all of its lustre. Had the dwellers in Italy not been of such calibre and quality as to create two literatures, Papal Rome had not grown to her gigantic proportions; possibly had not grown at all. The blood of her body was the mental pith whereof literature is at once the index and the embodiment; while out of the grandeurs and beauties and subtleties, whose purest expression is poetry, were woven her fascinations. Virgil and Ovid and Livy and Lucretius were as much her necessary antecedents, as were Dante and Petrarca and Boccaccio her concomitants and unconscious auxiliaries. Spirituality, the essence of elemental religion, is the life of the higher poetry, which, through the corroborating sympathies of the human mind, readily resolves itself into the devotional. The Greek Poets, if they did not generate, were the foster-fathers who shaped into symmetry the Greek Gods. Isaiah and Job and the Psalms give to the Hebrew Bible its aërial force, whereby it rises above the material earth, drawing toward Heaven the thoughts of mighty nations.

But despotism brooks no rivalry; and as the supreme masters in literature carry men's minds into that highest region of thought wherein — in order to be the masters that they are — they must have had their being, Dante and Kant and Pascal and Goethe and Shakespeare are ever objects of jealousy to priesthoods. These, aiming at control of the inward sources of opinion, would like to thrust out of the way those who, by the breadth and strength of their thinking, beget and sustain that elevation and freedom of thoughtful range where men are above the plane of rituals, and are apt to look on ecclesiastical pretensions with feelings more akin to disdain than respect. Thence priesthoods, and especially the Romish, as the most compact, would maim and inthrall literature. They would dilute its marrow, which is independence; they would tether its life, which is freedom. To this end goes their indirect influence as well as their purposed action. And where there is not the liveliest vitality in a people, at the core a soundness and vigor that will not abide stagnancy, spiritual aspiration is smothered, and the soul, lulled into contentment with such food as Cardinals and Bishops dole to it, creeps lazily on its earthly path, or sinks into a restless apathy.

In Belgium the obstacle to the kind and degree of development implied in the possession of a literature has not been territorial circumscription; and Palestine and Attica attest with unimpaired avouchment that neither largeness of territory nor of population is requisite for the culture and the concentration of thought needed for the production of immortal books. The chief obstacle has been geographical, the territory of Belgium being surrounded by overshadowing neighbors; an environment which, with the flatness of the land, has made her for centuries a battle-field for Europe, and thence, by destroying her political independence, has destroyed the first condition for mental self-subsistence, and has thus helped to tighten ecclesiastical bonds.

That sacerdotal sway cannot, with all its will and art, wholly smother the fire of a strong people's aspiration, we have evidence in the æsthetic creations of France and Italy, where the soul has wrought for itself wide and frequent vents through permanent literary monuments; and more emphatic still is this evidence in Spain, whose drama of the sixteenth century — so brilliant and rich an expression of the national life — bloomed and ripened amid the diversified diabolism of the Inquisition; and whence issued during the same period — to be an everlasting joy to mankind, domesticating himself among all the higher peoples — the dear, delightful, and most Christian and profound, "Knight of La Mancha."

Such an encompassment of a comparatively limited territory like Belgium — political hostility aggravated in her case on three sides by religious — has the effect of morally isolating a people, impeding that spiritual interchange which strengthens and refines the national sap through foreign infusions. The mental growth of nations, as of men, is furthered by the rivalries of association. People who stay at home get homely and provincial and self-sufficient. Human greatness, collective or individual, is nursed by collision. The shrivelling of the brain to insanity in solitary confinement is a proclamation by Nature of the need of companionship for mental health and expansion. Variety in companionship is as essential as frequency. If for a long term a set of people confine their intercourse to themselves they grow downward and dull.

My uncle had never been attracted to the scholarly enterprise of climbing the Teutonic tree to taste its literary fruit; yet he deemed that the opportunity should not be missed of ingrafting, through me and for my behoof, on the great parent stem, its Flemish offshoot. For myself, under the momentum of acquisition given me at Goettingen, I was ripe for a fresh study. Between my ears and the native speech around me there seemed now to be but a thin partition, through which I could detect the meaning of many words, only somewhat transformed by their garb; and I felt that a few weeks' work would level this partition and endue my semi-Flemish blood with the tongue of my mother's childhood.

My uncle was never precipitate, and when a new step was to be taken he proceeded with minute deliberation and a considerate survey of the whole field to be embraced. To engage a teacher of Flemish for a nephew was an untried procedure. Thoughtfully he cast about for the proper man.

Cunctative consultation was in this case superfluous; for, we being then in the country, there was but one man available — the schoolmaster of a neighboring village. To him accordingly application was made, and he agreed to undertake the new pupil.

"The village schoolmaster" of the old *régime*, even in a purely catholic community, was not of necessity a numskull. A routine, daily repeated through years, even in higher walks than subordinate pedagogy, dries the brain and deadens the spring of its action. But the possibilities of human nature are infinite; and many a man, humble and unambitious, so as to be content with a modest calling, bears within him a latent heat that keeps his faculties limber, blest with a resilience of soul that rebounds against the pressure of monotony, even when aggravated by the superposition of the parish priest, on the top of whom is a bishop, who carries a cardinal, on whose head stands the Pope, — under which sacerdotal load, to keep the mind alive and erect implies in the brain fine elasticity, and a private discipline like that in the muscles of the circus-hero, unbent beneath his pyramid of men. Of this elasticity my village teacher, poor fellow, had nothing. Nor beneath the weight above him was he smothered, any more than the frog is under the ground in winter: like so many, higher placed than himself, he lived in a semi-mental torpor. As behind him and his provincial vocabulary there sounded no Goethes and Schillers summoning me to a festival, we soon parted, the kindly woodeny man and I; and I dare say that to him the parting was not less welcome than it was to me.

X.

From Antwerp to Edinburgh.

WHEN I quitted Goettingen my aim was Edinburgh; and so, after a visit of two or three weeks to my uncle, I recrossed the Schelde, and, by the *diligence* which, two years before, had brought me so slowly and safely to Antwerp, made my way back to Ostend.

Ostend was then, and is still, and from its geographical advantages must ever continue to be, one of the readiest resorts of that open-handed class of Englishmen whose muscles are of so lax a fibre that they cannot keep their fingers clutched on guineas, but these will run out faster than they come in; which weakness subjects its victims to unseasonable persecutions from the close-fisted, who hoard more than they spend. To baffle these impertinences, the more liberal resentfully turn their backs on the gloomy shores of Albion, and for a term (often a long one) enliven the neighboring towns of France and Belgium with their leisurely free-and-easy presence. The suction of rank, which is ever straining at the ambitions of the untitled multitude, the magical oozing of oil from the hinges of fashionable doors on being touched with gold, the power of appearances, especially in England — these causes conspire to replenish this open-palmed breed,[1] many people being hereby incited to gauge their expenditure rather after the prodigality of their desires than the sordidness of their incomes.

Among those whom the peremptory British bailiff had chased into exile, was pointed out to me a *ci-devant* dandy, who figured conspicuously in the brilliant London "seasons" of 1814–15, and had been a college friend and afterwards comrade of Byron. Had these been his sole merits, hardly would my looks have been called toward him. But Fame, with her glittering finger, singled him out because his fingers had been linked in subtle work with those of one of her wealthiest heirs. He had written two lines in one of the stanzas of "Don Juan." This was Scrope Davies.

The King of Dandydom of that epoch, Beau Brummell, was likewise constrained to transfer his royal residence to Calais. Some one inquiring about him, a wit answered, that he spent all his time between London and Paris. To save his latter years from utter want, a petty consulship in one of the coast-towns of France had been given him. Being (cruelly) dispossessed even of this,

[1] For a characterization and panegyric of them, see Charles Lamb's exquisite essay on *The Two Races of Men.*

his remaining days were steeped in poverty, and at last "his realmless eyes were closed" in a madhouse.

Among my fellow-lodgers at the hotel was an Englishman, who, in the thirty odd years that he had been growing, had so seconded the saps of nature that his motions had a leopard-like grace of latent strength. He was a middle-class man without a liberal education; was six feet high, with slightly falling shoulders, and, without corpulence, had what is a strong point in the build of horses, called "a good barrel," with wide hips, so that the outline of his figure approached that of a woman. His head was not large, his countenance open, with regular unfleshly features that lent themselves readily to a laugh. His straight brown hair was slightly streaked with gray. We took to one another at our first meeting, and during my enforced tarry at Ostend were inseparable.

Man solitary were man no-man. Only through close union, multiform coöperation, can men be educated into manhood. The idea conveyed by the great word HUMANITY could not be ripened, or even reached, by the mere presence on the earth of millions of men, unbound by the interlacing bonds of limitless thought and thought's first-born, cumulative industry. Hence, infinite are the resources of nature for drawing men together. For the complex whole even of so incomplete a development of humanity as is our present civilization, the attraction of like unto like were all insufficient. Through endless combinations of unlike with unlike result, in the social and the political and the æsthetic and the scientific spheres, refinements and delicate complexities and subtle excellencies. For effective coöperation there must be affinities; but these are often latent and impalpable. As each planet, so each individual man has his atmosphere. Two atmospheres may intermingle ere the individuals have even spoken together. Interior correspondences sometimes melt outward incompatibilities. Individuals as diverse in their mental wants and ambitions as I and my transient comrade at Ostend, are held together through years by an inward inscrutable attrahent force, the unselfish to the selfish, the genial to the unimaginative, the quick-witted to the slow.

I did not learn the name of the Englishman, nor he mine; nor did I know what his past was or his present, except that from words casually dropped by him, I inferred he had something to do with the cargo of the steamboat. One evening, walking together on the quay, I withheld him from yielding to solicitations to which masculine loungers at that hour were liable. The next morning he thanked me, and probably gave me credit for being without the circle of such temptations. At times, to be thought better than we are is an offset of unearned credits against the undue debits scored to us by the unjust and the uncharitable.

Ostend, except in the season of sea-bathing, is not a place the traveller cares to stop in longer than for a meal. As in 1825 passengers were not of so much account as in 1865, the few of us bound for England were detained forty-eight hours beyond the advertised time, by the collecting and getting in of the cargo, which consisted of heavy Flemish horses. By means of a huge derrick and ropes, pullies and a stout broad bandage of sail-cloth, they were hoisted from the quay, and then let down into the hold. It was comical to see their passive fright as each horse found himself lifted from his feet and swinging in the air.

After a prosperous run, we were landed near the Tower of London on a Sunday forenoon.

Choosing my lodgings from the same motive that Charles Lamb chose his, I went to the *New Hummums*, which, being one of the several hotels that front on Covent Garden, was near both the great theatres. By the like of me at the *New Hummums*, that is, by temporary lodgers in a city, whether from abroad or from the country, the theatres get pit and boxes filled so full, — a secondary cause of the flimsiness of the material furnished, visitors in a city, much more even than residents, going to the theatre to kill time; and for your time-killer the most acceptable entertainment is one that is superficial, rapid, titillating.

The primary cause of the worthlessness of the major part of what goes on the stage is, that the general public — who, as regards its mental food, lives mostly from hand to mouth — prefers that which is momentarily stimulating, at best quickly assimilable, that which busies the attention without tasking the thought; and such food being the most easy to furnish, it results that buyers and sellers combine to keep of inferior quality the supply for the dramatic market. Tradition and the name, more than the mental might of Shakespeare, retain some of his plays in theatric repertories; but, had *Hamlet* and the *Merchant of Venice* been discovered yesterday, unknown as Shakespeare's, and been offered by the finder as his own, would managers accept them, and, if accepted and performed, would they be applauded and repeated? Considering the character of the later successful contributions to the stage, and the parallel inaptitude of theatric audiences to thoughtful depth or poetic elevation, it may be doubted.

In human affairs there is a descending tendence, the animal and worldly man asserting himself restlessly, oppugnantly, against the human and spiritual; and Literature and Art, owing to this downward proneness, would run to irredeemable platitude and blight were there not a counteraction from the upward bent given them by the higher class of thinkers, who, with their sympathetic controlling power, reach the finer cords of humanity and make them vibrate in unison with their own, — men, through the cordiality of genius, so disinterested, that their life's happiness is joy in fresh thought, and their love is for the work and not for its effects.

There is no literature, in the purer sense, but through re-creation, through the transmuting vitality of the individual mind. Mere reproduction of nature, the imitating and daguerreotyping of actuality, is lifeless, or rather, the attempt to reproduce and imitate, for it can never be more than an attempt; and hence, genial men of power aim at a radiant interpretation of nature, a symbolic semblance of the actual, fidelity to the spirit which is attainable, not fidelity to the body which is unattainable. Thence they alone give us visions of the beautiful, while the work of inferior men who fail to do so — and their inferiority comes largely from this failure — is opaque and prosaic and transitory, and when at its best falls, moreover, short of the truth; for not only is work transparent and buoyant and poetically aglow through its beauty, but likewise more trustworthy, there being in the beautiful such heavenliness that the higher you lift a subject into its light the more truth you see and teach.

The Drama — uniting in its essence the best of both the Epic and the Lyric, and offering, through its possible high mimicry of the interplay of passion and action in real life, the freest field for poetic creation — has ever been a favorite form with the masters in literature, some of them even contenting themselves with its one domain. Æschylus, Sophocles, Calderon, Molière, and, after his full manhood, Shakespeare, wrote only dramas. From Milton we have a tragedy and a pastoral comedy. The greater part of the poetic works, both of Goethe and of Schiller, are in the dramatic form. To descend to writers who, although high, are not master-spirits, all the works of Corneille, Racine, Alfieri, are in this form. The foremost of the remarkable modern British outburst of poetic genius, Wordsworth, Coleridge, Byron, Shelley, have left dramas.

To fervent poets the dramatic form is so attractive because by means of it they can leap at a single bound right into the middle of the great arena of human action. To creative genius it is not the story, nor even the characters that make the story, that are primary, but through these the drama becomes the most effective medium of elastic thought and soul-felt feeling. A poetic drama tends to be finely grandly generic, deeply symbolic. Thence Goethe says of Shakespeare's plays, — "The reader seems to have open before him the immense book of fate, against which the tempest of busiest life is beating so as to drive the leaves backward and forward with violence."

On the other hand, the sensuous scenic resources

at his command enable the manager to give effect to dialogue which, if printed, no one would read, but which, presented to the eye and ear through living speech, with all the illusive accompaniments of the stage, has a momentary fascination to the mind of the multitudinous half-educated, who sit in comfortable luxurious passivity, more spectators than auditors. Thus theatres get to be factories, offering, for the most part, to the public mental wares that help them consume an idle evening, giving them a dollar's worth of sight and sound, signifying little.

A literary work that is highly imaginative and highly intellectual will be largely spiritual, for the imagination and intellect cannot rise united to their upper phase but through union with the deeper wants and aspirations; and thence, the enjoyment which such a work is capable of giving being at its fullest only in silent solitary communion, a drama of the highest range cannot be embodied on the stage in its entire power. Some of the finer essence escapes, or rather, is absorbed by the gross corporeal actuality. For the twentieth time I read the opening scene in *Hamlet* with unabated awe, which is much dispelled if, sitting in a box, I see the ghost enter in palpable bulk. But not only when, with his transcendent mastery, Shakespeare opens vistas into the invisible is he beyond sensuous representation, but throughout his pages, when reading him, we are at every moment drawn to introversion and meditation; and in these supersensuous moods we reap the best harvests from his exhaustless fields..

Charles Lamb, in his profound and subtle paper against the fitness of the tragedies of Shakespeare for representation, says, — "The reading of a tragedy is a fine abstraction." Yet is our English breed immeasurably beholden to the stage, not for being the interpreter, but for being the dispenser, the diffuser of Shakespeare; for, tens of thousands have annually come, and continue to come, into his powerful presence through the pit and galleries, and the boxes too, who, but for them would never have had the benediction of his light upon their heads; and thus by means of the stage he has performed, and performs his great function of an unresting educator of humanity. He who sees Shakespeare and does not read him cannot take in the whole of him; but he takes in much, and what is nowhere else to be had. It is Shakespeare's privilege that he can be brought but partially on the stage. The best actor can give you but a portion of *Hamlet* or *Lear;* while Rachel gave the whole of Corneille and Racine. As for the crowd of sentimental melodramatic tragedies, for them the actors do more than their authors.

Of Shakespeare's tragedies the most representable are the historic; for here we have a great reality aggrandized by being embraced within the realm of the beautiful, a momentous epoch, through masterly gifts, transfused with poetic color.

Julius Cæsar I saw at Covent Garden with Charles Kemble as Antony. What martial music resounds through this magnificent drama. In no other of Shakespeare's is there in the march of the verse more of what Coleridge calls "angelic strength." In the opening scene what a significant mingling of homely and sounding phrases. With so close a grasp are we held, so entirely are our faculties in a moment taken possession of, that the words tingle in our ears like voices from our own market-place. What a prologue — and yet advancing the action so rapidly — is the first act, and what a picture of republican Rome at her height of sway and grandeur, so broad and luminous is each scene and speech and sentence.

The soliloquy of Brutus at the beginning of the second act — in the simple lines what a colossal style, and what tragic sadness. This speech somewhat puzzles Coleridge, who, with his genial generous belief in the flawlessness of the Shakespearean mind, — looking everywhere for logical consequence and rounded consistency, does not enough allow for the broad, careless, but sure, naturalness of Shakespeare, who lets his personages, under pressure of varying moods, speak apparent contradictions, his aim being to present us a man mobile from feeling, not an argument built of consecutive dry facts for a judicial tribunal. The speech of Brutus to the other conspirators, "No, not an oath." Here are words aglow with a noble nature's purest fires, shooting into beautiful flames with the breath of poetic imagination. And his humane rebuke of the proposal that Antony fall with Cæsar: —

"Our course will seem too bloody, Caius Cassius. —
We all stand up against the spirit of Cæsar,
And in the spirit of men there is no blood."

No page even of Shakespeare throbs with a more truthful tenderness, a sweeter pathos, than the scene with Portia: —

"O ye Gods!
Render me worthy of this noble wife."

This drama is of heroic mould. With such historic stature and inward life are the personages indued by the creative mightiness of the poet, they move and speak like men whose being and function are exceptionally exalted. Contrasted with prosaic history, it is like wresting stiff jejune figures out of the tame sequence of an old *bass-relief*, to intermingle them in full, elastic, variegated movement.

What an orator speaks under the name of Antony. How easily the verse rises to the level of Cæsar: —

"Cowards die many times before their deaths;
The valiant never taste of death but once.
Of all the wonders that I yet have heard,
It seems to me most strange that men should fear."

——— "Danger knows full well
That Cæsar is more dangerous than he."

This great tragedy is a teeming abstract of the tumultuous epoch, — the short-sightedness of the conspirators, the fickleness and obtuseness of the mob, the cruel, cold selfishness of the triumvirs, the politic and military short-comings of Brutus and Cassius, — everywhere the insufficiency of men's foresight and will transparent beneath the invisible guidance above them, their stoutest purposes turned to futility and naught.

Englishmen and Americans cannot put into words, cannot grasp in thought, their obligation to Shakespeare. Through the possession, the ever closer possession, for many generations, of his high thinking, his subtle insight, his clear, infallible intuition, these have come to be absorbed into the tissue of our race, congenitally immixed in our blood, mind of our mind. At birth we are stronger and better than we otherwise should have been, because among the constituents of the mental atmosphere unconsciously breathed by our fathers and forefathers were the splendent intellectuality, the warm geniality, the large sweet humanity of Shakespeare.

Of the million of men living in London in 1825, but two are still alive to me, and much more alive to me now than they were while on the earth, — Lamb and Coleridge, alive through that continuous communicable power which genius imparts to the higher intellect. I may have been a fellow-partaker with Lamb of one of the feasts nightly offered by Drury Lane and Covent Garden. I may have been seated near him; and had his unfleshly face and person been pointed out to me, it were now a frequent pleasure to recall the bodily figure of one whose individuality and its literary fruit have been and are to me a gainful enjoyment.

I incline to look upon the letters of Lamb — delightful and enduring as are the "Essays" — as his cardinal literary bequest. In diction as pure as those of Gray, they are more variously idiomatic, less external, and at the same time more sparkling than his, a more cordial revelation of the inner man, with a wider and more sympathetic range, coming as they do out of a deeper soul, and with an imaginative halo about them entirely wanting to those of Gray. In communing with Lamb through his letters you have a conviction of security, derived from the transparent trustworthiness of the writer's personality, a personality at once solid and ethereal,— solid from its upright manliness, ethereal from free irradiation and subtlest intellectual play. While garnished at times with the maddest mirth, his letters are steeped in the unfading charm of a rare humor, the more captivating from being entwined with a rare moral culture.

Had I met in London my friend Watson, from whom I parted on the Rhine, I should almost certainly have seen Coleridge, and, having seen him and heard him talk, I should have been open to the fascination of his speech, and so possibly have become a weekly hearer of his great discourse, or even have gained the prerogative of more intimate pupilage; for I had no specific purpose in going to Edinburgh, and, having since found in Coleridge so much that is food for me, I can believe that I might have been arrested, at least for some months, in the neighborhood of Highgate, and thus have found, what was not to be had at Goettingen, genial introduction into the boundless, beautiful domain of æsthetics and criticism.

Lamb, with the significant playfulness characteristic of him, writes in one of his letters to Wordsworth: — "Coleridge is absent but four miles, and the neighborhood of such a man is as exciting as the presence of fifty ordinary persons. 'T is enough to be within the whiff and wind of his genius for us not to possess our souls in quiet." De Quincey thus opens the first of the four papers of his "Literary Reminiscences" devoted to Coleridge: — "It was, I think, in the month of August, but certainly in the summer season, and certainly in the year 1807, that I first saw this illustrious man, the largest and most spacious intellect, the subtlest and most comprehensive, in my judgment, that has yet existed amongst men." Wordsworth said of him: — "I have known many men who have done wonderful things, but the only wonderful man I ever knew was Coleridge." And to these I add another, worthy to be classed with them, likewise a friend of Coleridge, our own Allston. Visiting him in his studio at Cambridgeport in the year 1839, I purposely referred to his acquaintanceship with Coleridge. As though a light had been suddenly kindled in his brain, his spiritual face grew more spiritual, his eyes visionary, as if withdrawn from outward things by some great memory, and with voice lowered to a solemn key, he said: — "The greatest man that I ever approached."

Although, of course, unable then to know and measure Coleridge as could these his matured illustrious friends, so strong has since been my sympathy with his mind, and through that so great my obligations to him, that I am sure, had I in those young years come under the spell of the poet-sage, much would have been implanted in me, and I should have received an impulse which would have greatly advanced my culture.

Through the capacity — not always possessed even by the potent — of giving hospitable entertainment to the ideas of others, and the capacity, still rarer, of generating ideas himself, Coleridge was one of the master-minds of his prolific, agitated era. Poet, thinker, dialectician, this mastery endures through a triune power, so throbbing with thought and genius that the higher men imbibe strength from his contact. To Coleridge applies especially the term *spacious* of De Quincey, not solely because in the reverberating chambers of his splendid mind there was room for so much and such various knowledge, but because the themes he took up revolved in so wide an orbit, and were handled with a grasp so quick with spiritual life. Boundless is the plane of the spiritually-minded.

Coleridge loves to circle in the upper air. His habits of thought are so high that he approaches his subject from above. He descends upon it with a vision made piercing and illuminating by sidereal ranges. It is not so much that you are instructed by his opinions and judgments — sound and fresh though these mostly be — as it is that your faculties are expanded by the vistas of thought disclosed. He is ever throwing open shutters that lay suddenly bare new landscapes with broad foreground, and stretching afar to sun-lit reaches.

He says of Burke: — "Burke felt how much his immediate power was lessened by the very circumstance of his measureless superiority to those about him. He acted, therefore, under a perpetual system of compromise — a compromise of greatness with meanness; a compromise of comprehension with narrowness; a compromise of the philosopher (who, armed with the twofold knowledge of History and the Laws of Spirit, as with a telescope, looked far around and into the distance) with the mere men of business, or with yet coarser intellects, who handled a truth, which they were required to receive, as they would handle an ox which they were desired to purchase." A mind of the finest needs, philosophically and morally of the largest calibre, will not warp and dwarf itself into such compromises. Coleridge himself would not have condescended to them. I think he overrates Burke, who had, it seems to me, a fine Irish fervor rather than a deep, truth-solving warmth. Coleridge was more opulent in resources than Burke, and far more aspiring, and had a firmer setting in principles. His mind was more nourished by ideas. The prose of Coleridge has at times a swing and freedom as though it had been written in a state of exalted passiveness, as though, like his "Kubla Khan," it had been dictated by the invisibles.

Through affluence in the nobler sensibilities, Coleridge is among the high moralists of literature. Yet an eminent critic, Mr. Matthew Arnold, in his admirable paper on Joubert, says of Coleridge: — "He had no morals . . . the disesteem, nay, repugnance which his character may and must inspire." Coming from one, himself so worthy of admiration, these words, when I first read them, caused me pain, followed by a flush of indignation. Mr. Arnold, and all of his generation who are so happily organized as to be within the direct sway of Coleridge's teachings, are under too strong and continuous obligations to the truth-seeking thinker, the earnest Christian, that any one of them should clothe in these terms an adverse judgment. The relation of pupil to master should have softened the wording of such a judgment. But the judgment itself is harsh, and to my feeling unjust.

The sins of Coleridge were sins of frailty, not sins of lust or pride. With all his splendid endowments, from defect of will he sinned against himself, and through himself against his fellowmen, curtailing them of the full fruit of his gorgeous gifts. But did he ever with selfish calculation, or with any calculation, harness his great fluent abilities to a car that was to carry him into place or power? Did he ever attempt to blacken the character or prospects of a contemporary with anonymous ink? Was his bearing towards his poetic brethren distorted by envy or jealousy, or was he in any of his relations grudging and grasping, striving to get and not to give? Not only would he have prospered better, as lodger and diner, but he would have been less a mark for the shafts of contemporaneous calumny or of posthumous detraction, had he thought more of himself and his worldly interests; for the world takes care of its own; and it is more curious than comforting to observe, how ambitious self-seekers, if plausible and prudent, not merely attain their coarse ends of wealth, or fame, or power, but moreover, for a time at least, persuade contemporaries of their disinterestedness. Coleridge lived so much in the higher sphere that for the lower he took not thought enough for himself and his. Amid soul-nourishing meditations the temporary needs were neglected.

Lamb, in the letter to Wordsworth already quoted, thus alludes to the fatal opium: — "Coleridge is at present under the medical care of a Dr. Gilman (Killman?) at Highgate, where he plays at leaving off laud—m. I think his essentials not touched. He is very bad, but then he wonderfully picks up another day, and his face, when he repeats his verses, hath its ancient glory; an archangel a little damaged." De Quincey, while dealing very unreservedly with the infirmities of Coleridge, speaks of his "gracious nature." He cites and blames the borrowings of Coleridge, — which, from the vast range of his reading, no one was more fitted to detect, — and says of the "Hymn to Chamouni," which he calls "an expansion of a short poem in stanzas upon the same subject by Frederica Brun," that "by a judicious amplification of some topics, and by its far deeper tone of lyrical enthusiasm, the dry bones of the German outline have been created by Coleridge into the fulness of life." Whoever will take the trouble to look through a *variorum* edition of Milton (not to speak of later lesser poets) will learn — somewhat, possibly, to his surprise — how frequent, and sometimes how direct, were his obligations to predecessors. A close search into Hollinshed, Plutarch, and the novels and tales current in the fifteenth and sixteenth centuries would reveal countless passages that were "expanded" by Shakespeare. In the course of his comment on the liberties taken by Coleridge with the pages of Schelling, De Quincey says: — "Coleridge spun daily and at all hours, for mere amusement of his own activities, and from the loom of his own magical brain, theories more gorgeous by far, and supported by a pomp and luxury of images, such as Schelling — no, nor any German that ever breathed, not Jean Paul — could have emulated in his dreams."

That Coleridge, with his mental pockets full of gold, and with a mine in fee wherefrom he not only replenished his daily purse but enriched his neighbors, should now and then borrow a guinea, is a fact at which we should rather smile than frown, or, more fitly, pass by without special sensation, seeing what has been the practice of the highest, — a practice which may, with full ethical assent, be regarded as a privilege inherent in their supremacy, the free use of all knowledge collected and experience acquired, no matter when, where, or by whom, being a natural right of him *who has the genius to turn it to best account.* That in certain cases where acknowledgment was due it was not made, we may ascribe to opium; or to defects which broke the complete rotundity of such a circle of endowments that without this breach they would have swollen their possessor to almost preterhuman proportions, empowering him to "bestride the narrow world like a Colossus."

Let the truth be spoken of all men. Let no man's greatness be a bar to full utterance; but let temperance and charity — duties peculiarly imperative when uttering derogatory truth — be especially observed towards a resplendent suffering brother like Coleridge, suffering from his own weakness, but on that very account entitled to a tenderer consideration from those who are themselves endowed to feel and claim something more than common human affinity with a nature so large and so susceptive. Could but a tithe of the fresh insights he has given us be allowed as an offset against his short-comings, never, from any scholar of sound sensibilities, would a whisper be heard against his name. Under the coarse, rusty, one-pronged spur of sectarian or political rancor, or from the gnawing consciousness of sterile inferiority to a creative mind, plenty of people are ready and eager to try, with their net-work of flimsy phrases, to cramp the play of a giant's limbs, or, with the slow slimy poison of envy and malice, to spot and deform his beauty and his symmetry. To such, to the half-eyed and the half-souled, to the prosaic and the unsympathetic, be left all harsh condemnation of Coleridge.

For the living, not for the dead, are these inadequate words spoken. The writings of Coleridge — in tone high, refined, noble; in expression rich, choice, copious; in spirit as pure as the sun's light; intellectually of rare breadth and mellowness and brilliancy — are a healthful power in literature, their influence solely for good, warming, strengthening, elevating. As for Coleridge himself, his is an immortal name; and as he walks through the ages, his robes adjusting themselves with varying grace, in harmony with the mutations of opinion, his inward life will be ever fresh to his fellow-men, while his detractors will be shaken from him as *gryllidœ* from the tunic of the superb Diana.

Although not addicted to retrospective lamentation, at times regret will come up that I can now look back to personal contact with Coleridge in 1825 only as an unachieved possibility. Without then knowing its nearness or even existence, I passed close by a vein of finest metal, whence in later years I drew treasures, and which a turn in circumstances might have laid bare to me in glittering presence.

About the beginning of November I left London. Not having a companion to help me to see the much that was to be seen by the way, I made no division of the long route into comfortable stages, but booked myself direct for Edinburgh in the mail-coach, which, without stoppages, except for hurried meals, went through in forty hours. The journey of four hundred miles is almost a blank in my memory, and but for one or two incidents would have in it no place. At York, where we stopped for a meal, I ran to get a look at the great Minster, and when we passed the border between England and Scotland a Scottish fellow-passenger warned me to be careful now of my words when speaking to unwedded females, else, before I knew what I was saying, I might find myself married.

XI.

Edinburgh.

WHEN in Dresden with my uncle, the year before, we took tea with a lady whose son, and only child, was then in Edinburgh. His letters, from which she read us extracts, were as from one living in an Elysium. On the flood of her sympathy the mother was lifted beyond the dull realism of the Dresden day, to be borne to the happy shores of the Frith of Forth, where she enjoyed that purest state of human being which is attained by throwing one's self out of one's self into the life of another, — a state, by a blessed privilege, most attractively open to mothers, but which is reached even at a higher level than through self-merging in persons, when to the discovering of truth, and the exposition of the principles that are the robust offspring of truth, the whole mind, without individual aims or temporary purpose, is disinterestedly dedicated, its best life absorbed into the object of pursuit, the EGO having the supreme happiness of becoming means instead of end.

Transition from Goettingen to Edinburgh being already in my thoughts as a possibility, our hostess

— a lady of sprightliness of mind and geniality of manners — urged upon me the boarding-house which her son found so comfortable, writing down for me the address. The traveller to a new city knows what a lenitive it is to his feeling of strangeness if along with him in his brain he brings his lodging, in shape of a picture of it hung there by some friend, especially if, as in this case, the picture be of fairest colors. The morning after my arrival, walking out from the hotel, the long-cherished address led me into one of those streets in the "new town" that run eastward towards Leith, and, a little way down the slope, in a not unfashionable part of the city, I came readily upon the house. Finding a vacant room, I had my trunk brought, and was at once installed.

It was a private boarding-house into which without testimonial I should probably not have been admitted. Besides the family there were but two other inmates, and no room for more. One was a lawyer, a *writer to the signet*, a quiet, sensible Scotsman, about five-and-thirty, of medium height and frame, a man of few words, whom I judged to be competent and trustworthy; the other a wine-merchant, partner or agent of the great Frankfort firm of Mumm and Co., of about the same age and taller, — a restless, somewhat pretentious German, for a time domiciliated in Edinburgh, who was always ready to talk without having much to say.

The mistress of the house was an elderly orderly widow, thin and active, an industrious noiseless housewife, with whom lived a son of about thirty, a lieutenant in the navy, unobtrusive, gentlemanly; and a widowed daughter, two or three years younger, of good height and light figure, a clear brunette, with rich, black, abundant hair, large, soft, black eyes, and regular features put together in almost Grecian proportions, — a young woman of dazzling beauty.

Here was the Sun that for the young Saxon baron had lighted up Edinburgh into an Elysium, had transfused with grace and benignity the entire population, with its warmth had so spelled the sights, sounds, odors of the Cow-gate and the Cannon-gate that they seemed delectable and delicate, had even made the outpourings from upper stories (whereto late-walking innocents in the streets were still occasionally liable) odoriferous night-showers — such conjurers are the words and eyes of a beautiful woman. The hallucination was probably emblazed through the delight Nature has in mingling opposites of the same race, — thereby to freshen and strengthen the breeds of men, — the short with the tall, the nervous with the phlegmatic, the impulsive southern man with the deliberate northern, the Celt with the Teuton, and in this instance the fair-haired Saxon from the eastward of Europe with a sparkling brunette of the west.

But man, with his wilfulness and his conventionalities, is ever contravening and perverting the plans of Nature. Just after we left Dresden the mother received a hint from a friend in Edinburgh (but was he a friend of the human species?) whereby the Caledonian Elysium was suddenly blotted from her imagination, and the Frith of Forth turned into an Acheron, "black and deep." Hurrying, with all the speed possible to those slow days, she arrived just in time to snatch her son's progeny from the jaws of heraldic destruction.

To Edinburgh I brought with me two or three keys to open the gates that let a stranger into the precincts called "Society." And rightly so called; for in a certain stage of civilization the social principle displays itself in a refined luxuriance of flower and fruit. People meet, not as they do in the market-place, or on "'Change," or even as at a family-gathering, but for intercommunication along cords that are strung in a plane that lies above interests material, or personal, or professional.

Political society, the organization of men into the State, could not come into being by a mere balancing of interest against interest. In the continuous existence of a State is implied the presence, and not the presence merely, but the predominance at times, of feelings and wants that have a finer fibre than material needs, what I might term generic, catholic feelings, — feelings that enlarge the enjoyer of them, enfranchising him from himself. The selfish, the individual impulses, man has in common with animals: the unselfish, the bountiful, are his exclusively: they constitute him man, and through them it is that he is empowered to build, for his protection and fortification, the State, — a vast compact social edifice, — and to ennoble and beautify it with institutions and creations which, flowing out of the spiritual, tend to uplift his being and to make his life on earth unanimal.

This deep aspiring social principle, out of which grows the State, (the largest and highest combined creation of humanity, and the larger and higher according to the degree wherein it embodies a coördinated complexity,) and which draws men out of the little self into the large self, this finds its delicate expression, its bloom, so to speak, in what in common parlance is called "Society."

Nor think because an egotist or a sensualist may sit high in this upper circle, or frivolity and vanity there flutter with scented silken wings, that therefore this claimed superiority is a sham or a usurpation. Though friends prove false or cold, friendship is a sacred certitude: deep and broad is humanity, though men are so often narrow and base. As some people are more muscular than others, some more courageous, some more compassionate, and as indeed inequality as well as diversity in gifts is one of the indispensable conditions for the progressive success of an extensive community, there are some in whom the elements are more finely mixed, with whom culture has so wrought on innate endowment, that they rise easily to the higher, the more spiritual, plane of life, and have their joy therein. Custom, inheritance, wealth, ambition give them as associates others in whose nature the descending are stronger than the ascending affinities. But these Time is ever shedding back to the earth. The nerve, the lifting force in "Society," is in men who have wide range of intellect, large sympathies, desire for thoughtful rather than sensuous enjoyment, — men who go out of themselves into Plutarch's men, or Shakespeare's, through whom cathedrals are built, and philosophies framed, and poems written, and empires consolidated, and the grandeurs of Art achieved.

Canning used to say that at dinners lettered men were the best company, more acceptable than members of parliament or even ministers of state: there was better talk in them. Not book-makers did he mean, or even necessarily writers, but men who, like himself, love the finer literature for the delight it can give, and through that delight an inward power, — men whose knowledge of daily common life has been deepened and mellowed by knowledge of uncommon life, that, namely, registered by choicest spirits in expressions suitable to such registry, — men in whom culture is enriched by geniality. Unleavened by some of these, communities stagnate and have hardly a history. Charles Lamb's "Wednesday Evenings," the assemblages at Holland House, the breakfasts and dinners of Rogers — had there not been present the stuff to make these renowned, "Society" in London in the first quarter of this century had been unworthy of its name. And it was in a measure unworthy of it; that is, it was not the full expression, the bloom, of the deep social principle, because the men who made these meetings renowned, and who did so because they were truly the *élite* of their generation, were not duly prized by those whose rank and wealth enabled them to make their houses the centres of social reunion. From the sensuous tone, from "the downward pull of sense" in aristocratic houses, there lacked appreciation of and sympathy with the genuine leaders, the men of insight and reach, at once the sap and the flower of social life. Coleridge, in whose tongue there was that could have awakened a listening nerve even in the dull ear of fashionable apathy, whom it ought to have been felt a privilege to be allowed to caress, for whom the choice of the high-born and the high-placed should have been brought together to do honor to with delighted ears and deferential admiration, — Coleridge was neglected.

De Quincey relates the wrath of a friend of his,

a wit and capital talker, who happening to call on Young, the actor, (a second-rate performer, who forty years ago played first parts on the London boards,) "was left to cool my heels for some time in a room where were strewed on a table for scenic effect, cards of invitation to dinner-parties of grandee Lords by the dozen, and to the balls, routs, *soirées*, of countesses, ambassadresses and duchesses by the score, — ay, and all falling within a few days,— more than ever I shall have in my whole life." A man, refined and scholarly, of high taste in life as well as in books, would not care to waste himself upon the dinners and routs of earls and duchesses whose emptiness sounds so tuneless through the noise made about an ephemeral notoriety. But in a better-conditioned "upper ten," a circle would have formed itself where the tone would have been given, not by the vain, who live on the light laborious follies of fashion, but by people of some mental aspiration and solidness, and where, therefore, the well-read and the well-informed, the polished man of heart, the modest scholar, would all feel themselves warmed by congeniality, and not — as in mere fashionable assemblages — chilled by indifference and silenced by superficiality. Fashion is apt to despotize over "Society," vulgarizing and sensualizing it. Such a circle would rebuke and discredit Fashion, and for its physically and mentally unwholesome practices tend to substitute purer desires and moods more manly.

Legaré, — at once an eminent lawyer and a literary student, who with a full accomplished mind was an admirable talker, — coming back to the hotel from a dinner-party one evening in New York, thirty years ago, on being addressed — "You have had a capital dinner?" answered — "The dinner was good enough, but what people they ask to meet you." The fact probably was, that nobody had been asked to meet him, but his arrival in town having been heard of, he had been added to a company already invited. To make such a man a guest in an uneducated circle is an incongruity amounting almost to ill-breeding. A host may take a fancy to have a table full of millionaires; but suppose that from caprice, or misdirected good-will, or ostentation, a chair on the same day be given to a thought-whittling transcendentalist or a poet of the extreme ideal school, his talk — if his tongue could find speech in such an atmosphere — would sound to the other guests like the cry of migratory wild geese high over head, invisible in the dark autumn evening, and to him theirs would be as indigestible as bacon and beans to a butterfly. To bring such opposites together for mutual entertainment in close, inevitable proximity, were to both an indirect impertinence. To invite guests with utter disregard of any principle of assortment is a kind of disrespect. Some of the art expended in getting up a feast should be given to the choice and juxtaposition of the feasters, and not all of it to that of the dishes. The diners should be *composed* as well as the dinner. Pell-mell dinners, debt-paying dinners, are capital things for people who want to eat a good meal, but they have no place in the chapter of social æsthetics. The German students have a somewhat contemptuous phrase to describe the miscellaneous crowded entertainments occasionally given them by the professors. They call one of these *eine allgemeine abfuetterung* — "a general feed." At such a feast there is a livelier flow of abdominal than of cerebral juices.

The word educated I use in its widest sense, not limiting it to B. A.'s or M. A.'s, or to literary or scientific proficiency. Some men are better educated by converse and travel than some others by much reading. Artists, genuine artists, with little aid from books, have the best kind of education, that, namely, given by thoughtful productive practice under the inward light of the beautiful. Their minds become flexible and full through their high strenuous work, which puts their whole being into disciplinary motion. Practical men, too, whose range is in the broader provinces of endeavor, leaders in large undertakings, civil or military, get cultivated by action. It will be found, however, that, besides having had early training and initiatory nurture at some academic institution, the most alert of these have been too expansible, too wakeful, to keep their intellects and their hearts closed against the subtle spiritual authority of good books. Let all bethink them that, mind ruling on earth as in heaven, giving breadth and depth and buoyancy to communities, naught else but mind, mind schooled, enlightened, expanded, ripe not raw, can give interest, diversity, tone, dignity to social converse. Gorgeous upholstery in palatial apartments, perpetual profuseness in silks, laces, jewelry, the predominance of titles and privilege, all this smothers, deadens "Society." In the glare of thought coronets grow spectral and unreal; in the sparkle of wit diamonds even are lustreless.

On the other hand, the literary element will not necessarily purify and polish; for literature, like "Divinity," can be made a trade of, people working in it for bread, or fame, or power. There is a lower and a higher literature. Of the higher Joubert is the most perfect type I know. Devoting his life to letters, he yet published nothing; but so enriched and refined was he spiritually and intellectually through this devotion that he became, by means of speech, the illuminator of the best writers of his time. But although literature, thus pursued, purges and tempers and elevates, while it intellectualizes the pursuer, literary men even of the higher class are not at all times the best company. From mobility and sensitiveness they are liable to be untuned, to vibrate discordantly. The meeting of many of them together in mixed society seems to relax rather than to tighten their cords, or to tighten them too much for music. Jealousies, diffidences, reserves, so cool their fires that they give out no more light than the unilluminated. Moore, in his "Diary," mentions a London dinner where, besides himself, were present Wordsworth, Campbell, Crabbe, and other metrical magnates. Expectation was at fault to depict the interest and brilliancy of the party. It turned out downright heavy. Moore's last words about it are, "it was dreary enough."

When a youth under twenty, De Quincey, through his mental precociousness and his knowledge of Greek, had access to a literary coterie in Liverpool, members of which were Mr. Roscoe, the biographer of Lorenzo dei Medici; Dr. Currie, the biographer of Burns; Mr. Clarke, the travelled cultivated friend of Roscoe, and others of local literary name. But the soul of the meetings was a tailor. De Quincey says: — "It was a striking illustration of the impotence of mere literature against natural power and mother-wit, that the only man who was considered indispensable in these parties, for giving life and impulse to their vivacity, was a tailor; and not, I was often assured, a person deriving a designation from the craft of those whose labors he supported as a capitalist, but one who drew his own honest daily bread from his own honest needle, except when he laid it aside for drooping literati, who needed to be watered by his wit." Were there in social usages and arrangements more freedom and cordiality, human intercourse on its higher plane would be oftener enlivened through men of this stamp by jets from the deep fresh springs of Nature.

The tempting invitations of this topic, if yielded to, would lead me into a lengthened untimely essay. This only will I add, that the refinement, the adornment, the enlargement of the wants and habits which is implied in the existence of what has got to be designated "Society," is due chiefly to a broad, expansive, yet subtle feeling, which is one of the humanizers and amplifiers of man, namely, to the sensibility to the beautiful. It was observed by the phrenologists, that people who swing themselves up out of a lower social sphere into the highest have a large development of what in their nomenclature is termed the organ of ideality. The faculty which gives buoyancy and beauty to the conceptions of Shakespeare and Milton, which makes their work new and elastic, which makes it, in one word, creation, is the same that animates the higher social intercourse. In a really "good Society" the poetic element in human nature combines with the moral and intellectual to give grace and elegance to the substantial and the worthy. But there is ever a proneness — especially in the shifting generations of our changeful country — to disanimate society through the frivolities and vulgarities of fashion and the sensualities of expenditure. Like the suffocating effect of covering the body with soft wet plaster, luxurious externalities and superficialities stop up the moral pores whose free open function is essential to the play of intellect and heart.

After the union of Scotland with England, the only privilege of a capital left to Edinburgh was the independent Scottish Judiciary. Socially speaking this was much; a body disciplined and cultivated as would be the judges and lawyers of an intelligent, strong-headed people — an important segment of the united realm — forming a solid intellectual nucleus. Another good element was the University. In 1825 Sir Walter Scott was clerk in one of the courts, and John Wilson a professor in the University.

In a city, exempt from the undulations and palpitations of either commercial or manufacturing growth, this combined influence would be the more pervasive. In Edinburgh there was, and had been for several generations, a quiet tone of culture. From what I saw and heard, general social meetings were neither frequent nor crowded. Every day was not a feast-day; and for this the social current was the clearer. In large national or commercial capitals social conflux, by its unintermitted rapidity, ploughs into its continents and makes itself turbid. In Edinburgh the social stream was not cumbered by men who spend their lives in carrying the burden of their wealth; nor by others who spend theirs in carrying that of hereditary rank, which is mostly obstructive and oppressive to themselves as well as to their neighbors. The titled and landed Grandees of Scotland had long since gravitated to the vast British capital at the south. An unwilling resident of Edinburgh was an earl, a bachelor scion of a noble house (said to be lineally descended from Shakespeare's Macduff), who for some seasons had been a companion of the regal voluptuary George IV., when Regent, and in that luxurious interlude had so damaged his rental that he was now cast back upon his native Caledonian shore — a wreck left by the fluctuating floods of fashion to bleach and crumble on the lonely sands of provincialism. He was then well past fifty, stout, with a certain breadth of bearing and flowing showy style of dress, a not uncomely man, who would be best described in the words of a witty friend[1] of mine, who said of some one that he was "the residuum of a thousand good dinners."

One day at a dinner-party an elderly gentleman

[1] The late John L. H. McCracken, of New York.

broke forth — *apropos* to nothing that had been said — in a eulogy of Jefferson. I account for the abruptness and zeal of his allocution — for he addressed himself directly to me — by supposing that a life-long admiration had been re-warmed by the presence opposite of a countryman of the great American democrat; and that its utterance was encouraged by the belief that he would have a more sympathetic hearer than he could often find among educated Britons. Such an address, made to me, was a happy illustration of the profit of travel. Jefferson I had not only never heard praised, but hardly even named, by those I looked up to, but to be dispraised, and sometimes in phrases culled from that vigorous vocabulary the unshackled circulation of which is one of the tokens of freedom, and which when applied to our public men seems to make them grow, as does summer succulents the dirt heaped about them in June by the gardener. To the animated eulogist I made no reply, and if I did not accept all he said I received it passively, and carried away a new image of Jefferson, and an image which the same words from an American adherent would not have stamped: I was made impressible by the foreignness and remoteness of the speaker.

On another occasion, at an evening party, a Colonel in the British army, a Catholic, and married into one of the titled Catholic families of England, after some conversation about America, announced to me that in a few years we should have in the United States a military despotism. I say announced, for he spoke in that steady absolute tone he would have used to impart an incident the certainty of whose occurrence had reached him by private channel some hours earlier than its public promulgation through the post-office. This gentleman was the victim (and he has many fellows) of an interior domestic conspiracy, his religion, his profession, his social position and associations, all conspiring to pervert him on this subject from the conclusions of common sense and humanity, and to make him the persistent dupe of hopes and beliefs as flimsy as they were uncharitable. Such people believe against evidence, hope against history. To him the annual falsification was but an annual postponement of his expectations; and should he happen to have survived to the present day, his life through our four years of civil war will have been an incessant tremor of disappointment; and to him the success of the United States in maintaining its integrity against so gigantic a rebellion will have seemed a calamitous catastrophe — a success which involved in large measure the political liberties of Christendom for many generations. He was one of that class of heady, wilful, unballasted men who keep their hopes and opinions in a state of boneless babyhood by allowing them to be the playthings of their wishes.

At Goettingen I had heard frequently of the University of Edinburgh; in Edinburgh I heard little of it, and from personal experience learnt nothing. The only use I put it to was to attend a popular course of lectures on Chemistry, given by one of its professors, Dr. Hope, a large, portly man, dressed with refined finish, of a fluent, graceful delivery, and celebrated for his chemical manipulations in the lecture-room. His numerous audience was made up chiefly of ladies, to whom was due the presence of most of the other sex. Popular lectures when good, as these were, are efficient light-horse auxiliaries to the trained army of conquest over ignorance. Knowledge, coming out of the core of the mind, is the seed which perpetuates that whereof it is the product, and, as with vegetable prolification, a dozen grains are not thrown in vain to the wind if but two or three fall where they can take root.

The theatre of Edinburgh keeps a place in my memory through Mathews. He had just returned from his first visit to America, and was coining guineas out of this new harvest of fun. He opened with words to the following effect:—"Should there be any Americans present I beg that they will not take otherwise than in good part my attempt to entertain you this evening. I am going to treat them as I have often treated the Scotch, the Irish, and the English themselves." There spoke the gentleman; and it was the refinement of nature implied in such an opening that gave to the performances of Mathews their unique excellence. They were the poetry of the droll and risible. In my mind he has ever since lain embalmed in those words.

I can never forget his entrance on the stage as an American just arrived in England. With a very long cigar in his mouth, on his head a white, very broad-brimmed hat, dressed with a loose, careless, somewhat showy individuality, he was followed by a huge negro — blacker than any ink that I can buy — bearing on his shoulders his master's trunk. The American has just arrived at a nobleman's seat, and mistakes the servants' hall for the drawing-room. To the butler, whom he supposes to be my lord, he addresses loud, rapid comments on England, delivered with a free-and-easy disregard of place and person, which to the formal obsequious butler is the same thing as impudence. Warming with the self-complacency kindled by the comparison he draws between England and America, he rises to an impassioned panegyric on liberty, than which a finer sample of the "spread-eagle" style was never offered by the most magniloquent of fourth of July orators. Abruptly he stops, subsides suddenly in manner and expression, walks up to the gaping butler, and in the equable tone of earnest business and with the shrewdest of looks addresses him:—"Do you want to buy a nigger?"

Mathews related, and evidently had pleasure in relating, an incident that occurred to him in Baltimore. The first morning after his arrival a physician, to whom he had no letter of introduction, called on him, made particular inquiries about his health and dietetic habits, paid a short visit and took his leave. The next morning the visit was repeated, and was so every day during his sojourn. Supposing this to be a custom of the place, Mathews, on the day of his departure, offered his visitor a fee. This, with a smile, the Doctor declined, saying to him, "I must now explain to you the cause of my daily visit. There have been some cases of yellow fever in our city, and as I knew that this would be kept from you, I felt it a duty to see that you, a stranger and a public man, should not suffer from the concealment."

A young traveller should be peremptorily directed to see certain things and persons, purely as subjects of reminiscence—as deposits in the mind whereon the memory through life will pay a dividend. I went only once to the court of which Sir Walter Scott was clerk, to get a look at the author of Waverley, and that week he was absent beside the sick-bed of his dying wife. It were now a pleasant memory had I attended some of the lectures of Wilson. Jeffrey I saw but once, and then only in passing, as he was pointed out to me in the "outer house," or large vestibule to the courts in Edinburgh. With the will to know them I could have been introduced to both; and I now regret not to have made the slight effort necessary; for they helped forward their contemporaries, albeit they are not men to whose words one has recourse as to self-preserved stores of that inexhaustible fund supplied by the very few who are created to hearken so intently for truth that her throb tunes their best motions. May not this power of spiritual auscultation be the chief token of genius? In a critique, in I think the "North British Review," on occasion of the Memoir of Wilson by his daughter, he was finally characterized, with justice it seems to me, as a rhapsodist. And Jeffrey, quick, clever, versatile, had not the breadth and weight and fine verity for permanent literary mastership. On his page are kindled no fires to which after-generations can go back to light their torches. His blaze was for his generation; and a timely blaze it was that he and Sidney Smith and their venturous fellows flared over the British realm at the beginning of the century through the "Edinburgh Review," making visible and detestable many a monstrosity and tyranny of wrinkled custom and usurping privilege.

My companion in the "outer house" related the following anecdote. A young lawyer, a *protégé* of Jeffrey, a minor point of law having in the course of a trial been decided against him, had told the Judges with warmth that he was astonished at their decision. Hereupon the Bench refused to let him proceed, until he should have made them an apology. This he declined to do, and hastened out to find his friend. Jeffrey, on hearing the statement, said: "Leave the matter to me, I 'll make an apology for you"; and accompanying his irate colleague into the court-room, addressed the Judges as follows: — "My Lords, I am exceedingly sorry that my young friend here has allowed his temper to get the better of his tongue. He is young and unpracticed, and I beg that you will ascribe his hasty words to inexperience. For his future behavior I will answer; and I take on me to assure the Bench that when he shall have known your Lordships as long as I have, he will not be astonished at any decision you may make."

Into the saying of this there went a quick wit, but the wit we should never have had but that the sayer was a man of still more face than wit. Lord Bacon has an essay on boldness, showing what it can do and why it can do it. Bacon calls that boldness which, using a term more blunt and also more discriminative, we now call impudence. As affairs are yet managed on our earth, impudence is not so much the opposite of a virtue as its etymology might purport, and many things which, for the benefit no less than the amusement of men, ought to be said and done, would be left unsaid and undone but for that semi-shameless, procacious quality which prompts some to throw themselves forward when others hold back, — out of respects that for this saucy world are too dainty. The impudent help to keep the ball a-going, often picking it out of the dirt where cleanly hands would not reach for it. Thus they may be said to sacrifice themselves for the general weal; and although their motives be almost always personal and selfish, the results are sometimes public and good.

In the famous article on Wordsworth's *Excursion*, — the first in No. 24 of the "Edinburgh Review," beginning "This will never do,"— is exhibited but one of the two qualities so conspicuous in the speech to the court. The audacity stands in bold, shivering loneliness, uncountenanced, unwarmed by wit. As criticism the judgment given has long since been reversed in a superior court. Moreover, the article is self-condemned, being curiously self-contradictory. On page 2 you read :— "The case of Mr. Wordsworth, we perceive, is now manifestly hopeless." Page 3 : — "And making up our minds, though with the most sincere pain and reluctance, to consider him as finally lost to the good cause of poetry, we shall endeavor to be thankful for the occasional *gleams of tenderness and beauty which the natural force of his imagination and affections must still shed over all his productions.*" The lines I have italicized are inconsistent with the "hopelessness" of Mr. Wordsworth's case, and with the following on page 4: — "The volume before us, if we were to describe it very shortly, we should characterize as a tissue of moral and devotional ravings, in which innumerable changes are rung upon a few very simple and familiar ideas: — but with such an accompaniment of long words, long sentences, and unwieldy phrases; and such a hubbub of strained raptures and fantastical sublimities, that it is often extremely difficult for the most skilful and attentive student to obtain a glimpse of the author's meaning; and altogether impossible for an ordinary reader to conjecture what he is about." Toward the close of the article, after many passages "of interest or beauty which we have quoted, and [or] omitted to quote," the reviewer writes on page 29: — "When we look back to them, indeed, and to the other passages which we have now extracted, we feel half inclined to rescind the severe sentence which we passed on the work at the beginning." And this — had he been able to read aright these very passages, that is, with imaginative insight — he would have done. But the sin of the article is in its tone, a tone in which no high pure criticism can be written. To characterize this needs plain words. It must be called conceited, malapert. It is that tone which is so imitable and is so much imitated, because it is a mask readily handled to hide shallowness and lack of native resource. Now Jeffrey was neither shallow nor lacking in resource — except when he undertook to confront critically a great imaginative Poet: this was a task above his powers; and, through the flippant arrogance of this paper and in the very folds of its assumed ease, there is discernible a semi-consciousness of his inadequacy. His was not a mind to accompany Wordsworth as he mounts on the strong steady pinion of an idealizing thoughtfulness, lifting trite themes into the empyrean of poetic meditation to make them shine with unexpected lustre. His was not a mind into which flow

> The tides of full emotion, swelling deep
> The raptured brain, and brimming thoughtful eyes
> That outward glow with visionary joy.

Few are the minds of this calibre and composition, and none others are competent critics of highly imaginative poetry, on its first appearance. When such poetry has been long before the public, and has in some measure "created the taste whereby it is to be judged," then critics of less original gift become so disciplined as to cope with it. The Poems of Byron and Scott were pretty fairly estimated the year they were published: those of Wordsworth and Shelley not for many years.

So much easier, and thence more common, is it

to reproduce from the memory than to produce from the imagination, that most writing, verse as well as prose, is but the former, each reproduction modified — in the best cases freshened — by the individuality of the writer. Critics, writing under the same tyranny of memory as other pen-wielders, when original work comes before them few can appreciate and the most are even repelled from it; and not until its worth has been stamped by those minds which, having in themselves creative power, put themselves instantly into friendly relation with originality, does the circle of clever critics, and the general mass who adhere to them, accept the revelation of new thought and beauty.

I had spent in Edinburgh an aimless, rather idle winter, reading but not studying. What a young man, especially one who has in him any literary faculty, at that age needs, is helpful fellow-feeling, — a somebody, ahead of him in years, to feel with, for having himself felt, his wants, aspirings, misgivings, imaginings, hesitancies, hopes, doubts. But out of a score is there one whose fortune throws upon him the blessing of such a friend? not to repress and prohibit, but on the contrary a Mentor trustful, far seeing, who will inspirit his boldness, will fan his enthusiasm, encourage his audacities, if they have sprouted, and if they have not, tempt them out with judicious sympathy. But the culture of a man for his own high sake, for the best there is in him, this is not the aim of the institutions and influences which a youth entering life finds about him: these aim to fit every one to be a worldling who will help the world forward in its worldliness.

Lacordaire, in his "Conférences de Toulouse," has a beautiful passage on spirituality and poverty: "God, who toward man has been prodigal of spiritual gifts, who has put no bounds to peace, love, heavenly blessedness — an infinite treasure whence each of us may draw at will, God has shown himself grudging of material goods. Food and raiment he has measured to us with a parsimony which would be frightful, had it not its cause in what I have said of the blessedness of poverty, and if there were not in material abundance a vivacious principle of corruption." As easy were it

"to hold a fire in his hand
By thinking on the frosty Caucasus,"

as for a man who keeps a bank-book to believe in the blessedness of poverty. How will you convince him that fresh dividends are wormy? Insolently deaf is he to the text which declares that it is hard for a rich man to enter the kingdom of Heaven, — a text profound, faithful, implying, as it does, the tyranny, acquired by habit, of the sensuous over the supersensuous, the rich man's thoughts, feelings, acts, becoming in most cases absorbed either in the getting and piling of the grosser materials of life or in spending what has been piled for him.

> "The world is too much with us; late and soon,
> Getting and spending, we lay waste our powers;
> Little we see in Nature that is ours;
> We have given our hearts away, a sordid boon!" *

On the other hand, the poor — those at least whose lot is cast above tropical or semi-tropical latitudes — are so pressed by the divine parsimony in material goods, that, like the mammonish gold-heaper, their best life is necessarily absorbed in getting food, lodging, and raiment; and by this pressure the more weakly organized of them are crushed into vice and crime, making a beginning of hell here on earth — a pendant to that made at the other end of the scale by the rich sensualist.

Nor is it easy for a rich man to enter the kingdom of Literature, that is, the upper kingdom; for, the aggressive materiality and worldliness engendered by money or worldly power, which film the spiritual vision, darken or obstruct the poetic. Had Shakespeare, in place of Sir Thomas Lucy, been born the proprietor of Charlecote, would the world have enjoyed what is now its greatest literary possession? Had Dante, instead of being discomfited and exiled, been, from his thirty-fifth to his fifty-fifth year the triumphant chief of the Tuscan Ghibellines, ruling Florence with the vigor and

* Wordsworth.

talent and patriotism which must have shone in his administration, Tuscany might have prospered and predominated, but Italy and Christendom had been impoverished by the want of the *Divina Comedia*, truly, in another sense than that he named it, a divine piece of human work. Deeply set out of sight are the springs of human motion, have subtle untraceable activities and torpors, elasticities intangible, incalculable.

De Quincey, when he was already well entered on manhood, lost, through generosity and unthriftiness, his patrimony. Surely what was the cause of a blessing to his generation and many following generations, cannot be deemed a misfortune to himself. The loss thrust him back on his large dormant resources; and fecundities, which in the De Quincey of eight hundred pounds a year would have only borne flowers to beautify and perfume a private circle, have in the penniless De Quincey yielded a score of the best volumes of English prose.

One refuses to believe that a lofty nature like Milton could have been buried under a pile of gold, however huge; but if not utterly smothered, his deep pure breathing could not but have been obstructed and fouled in an atmosphere of material superabundance. As it was, by the pressure of external circumstances the poetic voice was hushed in him for a very long period; and while we honor and revere the earnest gifted man who to the cause of freedom dedicated nineteen years of life, taken right out of his middle manhood, and while we immensely prize the practical coöperation of such men, enriching as they do by their active presence the meagreness, and ennobling the meanness, of ordinary politics, we yet cannot help thinking (albeit retrospective plaint is the emptiest of idleness) that in those marrowy years such a genius might have wrought what would be still more precious than even his grand sonorous prose. When Uhland was elected to the *Chambers* of Wirtemberg, Goethe said: — "Many a man will make as good or a better legislator than he, but Germany has but one Uhland the poet."

In the dazzling constellation of recent British genius there is not a wealthy member. Scott began poor, and when, through his facile fertile pen, his annual income grew to many thousands, he fell a victim to riches and the earthly ambition they stimulated. Literature has no more sorrowful spectacle than the stalwart upright man in his latter days, the spirit heaving against the weight laid on it by the flesh, — an unnatural, unbearable struggle, from which the spirit soon freed itself, to go up to where there are no baronial families to be founded, no tempting commercial partnerships, no misleading popularities. Byron, born in the station of Wordsworth, would have been called a man of means, and what had been the result, poetically or unpoetically, it is not easy to estimate in one so wayward, violent, ill-balanced. But Byron was not a rich yeoman, and he was a poor lord. How twenty or thirty thousand pounds a year for the peer to spend would have modified or diluted the poet one can hardly say; but we may believe that wilfulness, self-indulgence, and worldly ambition, would have run into the artificial channels scooped by torrents of gold, and that the poetical outcome of his life would have been less than it was. Poetic genius, when strong in a strong nature, will, against outward hindrances, burn itself a vent; but it must have air to breathe, and our position is, that if the air be loaded with effluvia from the rankness of worldly power or worldly expenditure, it is not a fit medium for the clear musical voice of the higher literature. Poetry, however strong and spontaneous its flow, requires for its due embodiment strenuous, concentrated, conscientious work; and men, beset by the opportunities and flatteries of luxury and sensual enjoyment, become unbraced for this sort of close self-merging effort. A born poet, nursed in a hovel, will much more surely surmount the obstacles to his poetic growth incident to that birth than he will those that would confront him in a palace.

Wordsworth, Moore, Coleridge, Campbell, Keats, were all poor. Wordsworth, from his early to his middle manhood, had a succession of windfalls; as if the Muses had plead with Providence to insure against the impediments of a pinching poverty one who began life by formally dedicating to their highest service his whole rare being, and who with all his gift — and perhaps partly on account of its elevation and purity — would not for long years draw from his verse much pecuniary meed. Coleridge was too poor; and how could he ever be so commonplace prosaic as to make money — the wide-ranging, sublime, uncompromising seer and talker. But he had kind friends — blessed be their memory — and among the earliest the Wedgewoods, who settled on him an annuity, which was a steady stay to him through life, and for which their names will shine in literary annals long after the last plate of their famous ware shall have crumbled. Shelley, though heir-apparent to a rich baronetcy, never had, during his too brief manhood, more than a thousand pounds a year; and this, with his giving nature, was only enough to loose him from the galling yoke of uncongenial work, leaving his aspiring tendencies free to obey their bent. But him it is harder than any other to conceive of as subdued or disabled by gold.

Goethe's father designed him for the law; but as easy were it to suppress in an Arab courser all gaits but the walk, as to have made the main current of Goethe's life run in the slow conventional channel of German jurisprudence. The irrepressible creative power burst forth early in Goetz and Werther; and the precocious judgment and prophetic instinct of the young Duke of Weimar (scarcely twenty years of age) seizing upon the author as a helper and friend, Goethe found himself in the at once studious and active retirement of Weimar, free to follow the leadings of his dilating adventurous mind. The death of his father brought him in after years a patrimony, which in Frankfort would have been a snug burgher's portion. Goethe's troubles came from within. The richer the organization, the greater the liability to internal conflicts. Men of wide sympathies and fine temperament suffer through their susceptibilities — secret inward sufferings, unknown often to those nearest to them. For the full play of his genius Goethe had what he needed, — a certain ease as to outward things. This he needed more than Schiller who, with less disturbance from inward causes, was at the same time less hindered by straightened circumstances than Goethe would have been. But for Weimar's noble Duke, the illustrious Carl August, Schiller might have been so straightened that his poetic growth would have been stunted. As it was, he was compelled to expend on mere bread-work (to use a German phrase) more nervous fluid than was wholesome. To be sure, he never was reduced to the straits of poor Coleridge, who at one time had to write sermons to sell, a stipulation in the contract being that they must be kept intellectually down near the dull level of the buyers, who were to preach them as their own. Think of that as a morning's task for a Coleridge! Think of a surcharged thundercloud commanded to withhold its lightning!

XII.

From Edinburgh to Paris.

On Monday the 22d of May 1826, an hour after sunrise, I was on board the steam-packet *Brilliant*, bound from Leith to Aberdeen. We hugged the shore, not on account of its beauty, for, with brief exception, it was notably flat and barren. Arriving at six I put up at Dempster's Hotel, where from the friend, on whose invitation I had come to the north of Scotland, I found a note saying he would drive in for me the next day. This was Colonel Wood (now General Sir William Wood) of the British army, who, having been wounded at the battle of Bladensburg in 1814, was left in the village on the hasty retreat of the invading army after the capture of Washington, and whose nature made him believe that for some kindness shown him by several families of the neighborhood he never could be sufficiently grateful.

I had time before supper to view the town, get a look at the County Hall, note the rich shops of Union Street, and the air of material prosperity, and to fancy that the physiognomies of the people were more pleasing than those of Edinburgh. Perhaps they were only different. After a supper of lobster and haddock I had toddy and talk with two or three sociable Scotchmen, who prefaced their first draught with the standing local toast — "The town and trade of Aberdeen."

Colonel Wood resided near Banchory, a small village on the Dee, about sixteen miles west of Aberdeen, in the neighborhood of half a dozen other families, all living in that easy elegant comfort which is a feature of the rural life of the British gentry, and, attained through centuries of gradual, civilizing, refining progress, is maintained by the accumulation and diffusion of culture and capital. Nearly opposite, on the other side of the shallow salmon-haunted Dee, lived General Burnet, who was an ensign with Burgoyne when captured at Saratoga in 1777. At his table I noticed an old-time custom. Between the guests were silver tankards filled with ale, each tankard for its two neighbors, one carrying to his lips the right side, the other the left.

I accompanied my kind host and hostess on a visit for a couple of days to the seat of Mr. Farquharson Innes of Monaltry, about fifteen miles further west, where we found ourselves in the Highlands. A substantial, roomy mansion, amid wooded hills and dells, in a wild forest that almost encroached upon the walls; a cordial hospitality; billiards with young ladies; opposite me at the dinner-table a picture with figures of life-size representing one of the ancestors of the family about to mount his horse to start on some storied expedition, with one foot in the stirrup, by the cruelty of the painter fixed for centuries in that momentary constraint; such are the memories of that highland visit. This life in the country for eight or ten months of the year, without rural seclusion and its consequent rusticity and provincialism, is a healthful ingredient in English existence. In the young it nourishes health, moral and physical; it keeps both mind and body aired.

On the second of June my hospitable host went with me back to Aberdeen, where we dined with the County Club, Major Hay in the chair. In a company of forty or fifty, five or six were named to me, hardy, hale gentlemen, past middle age, who, having made fortunes or competencies in the West Indies, in South America, in the East Indies, at the Cape of Good Hope, had come home to dear old Scotland to enjoy the fruits of their distant sagacious toil. The enterprise of her citizens is ever seconding the large, deliberate, inexorable ambition of her government to make all the continents and oceans of the globe tributary to the wealth, and I may add, to the knowledge of England; so that "this sceptered isle," "this precious stone, set in the silver sea," is, to Englishmen at least, the centre of the earth, for from it run intellectual, industrial radii to all segments of the earth's water-bound circumference.

At a certain stage of the dinner I became tremblingly alive to what was coming. In a few moments I should have to face as speaker a strange audience. Some of my readers have doubtless gone through this ordeal. Whoever has or has not, let him read Hawthorne's chapter on Civic Banquets in "Our Old Home." After him to attempt to describe the proceeding and its sensations were a preposterous presumption.

Toward midnight I was in the mail-coach that was to carry me to breakfast at Dundee, through Brechin, and through the almost nightless night of this high latitude in June, where darkness has hardly night enough to build its deeper caverns. Thence up the Tay by steamboat to Perth, where I spent an agreeable Sunday, having a letter to Dr. McFarlane, Jr., who showed me the beautiful environs of Perth. Macpherson, whom Wordsworth calls the "sire of Ossian," had been tutor in the family of Dr. McFarlane's grandfather. The Doctor said he was a proud man, keenly ambitious of literary fame, and hence was glad to have the Gaelic origin of Ossian doubted, purposely keeping in obscurity the evidence of this origin. But aged persons were still living who remembered when these stories — before their publication by Macpherson — were told in circles of the young; and so diffused and minute was the knowledge of them, that some of the listeners would be sure to correct the narrator, if the smallest item, or even a word, were omitted. Now Wordsworth says of Ossian that "the characters never could exist, the manners are impossible, and that a dream has more substance than the whole state of society as therein depicted." He pronounces the whole book to be "a phantom begotten by the snug embrace of an impudent Highlander upon a cloud of tradition."

On Monday morning I was at Stirling, and after having walked to the castle and despatched my trunk to Glasgow, took a gig to drive through a beautiful country to Callender, and thence to Stewart's inn on Loch Akray. Toward evening I walked through the Trossachs. The guide drew my attention to what I should otherwise not have seen, so secreted was it among bushes and boulders — a small hut, now partly demolished, where whiskey had been manufactured, to be sold without paying the excise, an inland hole for smuggling. The whiskey of this region is noted for its flavor and quality. What is alcohol? The Dictionary says the Arab word means essence or spirit. Essence or spirit is life, concentrated life; but alcohol is concentrated death. Is it from barren one-sidedness, from its being a forced exudation from, a compulsory extract out of, saccharine, and therefore nutritious substances, that it intoxicates, that is, poisons? Is it because it is counternatural, a meddlesome perversion of God's gifts, because the use of it implies a lusting after forbidden flavors, a morbid craving for more life than we can bear, like an impious sporting with the blinding, shattering lightning? Has it some recondite, not wholly obliterated, affinity with good, such as Satan had with God? It certainly is a Devil who with lies and flatteries has won the free range of our Eden. Does its venom come from its rejection, through distillation, of all wholesome elements? The more dephlegmated it is, that is, the freer from aqueous particles, the purer it is. Hence, in part, its enmity to the tissues of the human body, they being three fourths water. Full of fire and explosiveness, rightly did the poor Indians, whom it has slain by myriads, call it fire-water. Whence its terrible attractiveness? Like the latent heat in the blood which, when it rises above a certain grade, consumes instead of vivifying, is alcohol a principle of life carried to a consuming degree? When people are languid or cold, by it they may, for the moment, be inspirited and warmed. When the springs of life are weak or worn, through the weight and wear of feelings disappointed, wounded, crushed, men try to lighten the brain with the fumes of alcohol: they take it to their inmost confidence as a friend! These lines, applied to a woman in Shelley's mysterious *Epipsychidion*, do they not describe this insidious vegetable demon?

"Flame
Out of her looks into my vitals came;
And from her living cheeks and bosom flew
A killing air, which pierced like honey-dew
Into the core of my green heart, and lay
Upon its leaves; until, as hair grown gray
O'er a young brow, they hid its unblown prime
With ruins of unseasonable time."

We are wisely taught that waste is criminal. As children we are told to throw even refuse bread-crumbs where the birds may get them. To turn life-nourishing grain into life-wasting poison, what a thousandfold crime! Well were it for humanity if, like the unroofed hut in the Trosachs, all buildings on earth, where poison is brewed from food, could be made desolate. Only then will they become desolate, when men's lives shall be so full of true stimulants that they will no longer thirst for false ones. And that blessed time is yet to be.

We were more than two hours in a row-boat on Loch Kathrine, landing for a few moments on Ellen's Island, where I plucked a wild hyacinth. From the western end of the lake a walk of five miles brought us to Loch Lomond, in time to hit a steamboat. Passing through the whole length of the lake, and by Dumbarton rock and castle, we entered the Clyde, arriving at Glasgow at eight, after a delightfully well-spent day. The next morning a river-boat took me down to Greenock to go on board a sea-boat that was to start at noon for Liverpool.

Sitting in the evening below deck with a book, the captain and two or three passengers — not conceiving that an American might be so near — assailed my passive ears with abuse of the United States, talking boastfully of the *Shannon* and *Chesapeake*, and declaring, that behind cotton-bales school-boys could have defended New Orleans. The talkers were of that uncultured class among whom the weeds of prejudice and provincialism grow into a choking rankness. International, like individual, fault-finding is often but a coarse manifestation of what may be termed a conservative egotism. The strong individuality (nobody abuses weak people) of a neighbor seems to threaten mine; that there is a difference in our natures is a kind of reproach to me. The individuality of a man is his all; it encloses his whole being. Any opposition to it — and a character prominently variant is a latent hostility — makes him gather himself up defensively as when his body is menaced. And so with nations, except that here the discordancy is more permanent and defined. Were individuals or nations all exactly alike, there would be, there could be, no antagonism; and then life were but a sleepy languor, an unimpassioned platitude, a changeless, tuneless tautology. Inequalities, rivalries, are ingredients of development. The more marked and abundant the inequalities, and the more various and active the rivalries in the bosom of one people, or between several peoples, the wider and manlier will be the welfare and the more assured the progressiveness.

An involuntary eaves-dropper, — like myself in the cabin of the *Majestic*, steam-packet between Greenock and Liverpool, — enforced to listen to the various European nations while giving to international dislikes and antipathies that broad untempered avowal which is apt to issue from such a knot of frank racy middlemen as I was overhearing, might conclude that a strong element in the mutual feeling — not between the inhabitants of any two nations merely, but between any one and all the rest — is a chronic hate, and that not only do Frenchmen and Englishmen interdespise (to borrow a coinage of De Quincey's), but that they both unite with the Spaniard and the Italian in aspersing the German, the German giving each of them as good as he sends ; and so on all round the map. And so on all through each section of the map, the southern Italian being ever ready to scowl at the northern, the Norman Frenchman harboring toward the Gascon a sentiment any thing but purely fraternal, the Scot and the Englishman eying each other jealously. So too among different towns of the same land, even among different portions and streets of the same town. All the countless differences and inequalities among nations, sections, and individual men, Nature works with for her ends of productiveness and advancement: all the colors and shades of color that dye and play through the human heart she combines to create the far-shining stimulating white light of Christian civilization.

I had come to Liverpool to meet my father and sister, and the era of ocean steamships not being yet entered on I waited a week for their arrival. On the 18th of June we left Liverpool, making our first stage to old Chester, the second to Wrexham. The country was alive with the stir of a parliamentary election. From Wrexham to Ellesmere (Saxon for great water) we drove in a barouche with an electioneering placard pasted on it, —"Independence, &c., &c.;" a proclamation, prolonged through a thousand years, of Anglo-Saxon freedom; for England, ever since, under the guidance of the great Alfred, she emerged from barbarism, has been a land of popular power. However limited the number of the electors, however selfishly dominant at times the nobles, however dictatorial some able unscrupulous king, the individual Englishman has always — except during short historically critical epochs — possessed, as to personal movement, speech and endeavor, exemption from oppressive disheartening central control. In the deep throat of the race there has ever lain a leonine growl of manliness, ready to warn executive encroachment. It is a strong breed, compounded and compacted out of many stems, slowly unfolding itself into shapelier forms and combinations. For more than a thousand years English history is a gradual growth, an expansion, a gain earned by incessant sturdy effort under the lead of instinct and insight. Robust fruitful natures have ever abounded on English soil. Out of the multitude have arisen in every generation strong, apt men, nervous centres, absorbents and distributors of living energies. A stout heart has always kept the brains of Englishmen warm with a courageous current. With what a will they cut one another's throats through many generations on a hundred civil battle-fields. That headsman, with the axe turned toward the prisoner, what a recurrent terrible figure he is in English annals. With what calmness and dignity their nobles laid their heads on the bloody block. With what duteous devotion, with what unflinching fortitude, their martyrs walked to the stake. There is no better sign of a rich race than that it throve on so much killing. The axe and the sword seem to have been means of mental fecundation. And their kings! Are the chapters of any other history headed with such a roll of regal puissance? Alfred, warrior, scholar, lawgiver, the model of regal manhood; and Richard, the lion-hearted Crusader; and the victorious first and third Edwards, with their martial Black Prince; and the valiant Henrys, the Second, the conquering Fifth, and the fierce, able, big-headed, uxorious Eighth, the wife-slayer; and his great daughter, who, happily for England and Christendom, reigned a half century, — the wilful, jealous, sway-loving, sway-worthy Elizabeth, girt with such a belt of men as sovereign on earth never was before or since, the virgin Queen, for who was large enough to be her lord, save the crownless King, Oliver Cromwell. What a pair!

The Stuarts we can only look upon as a providential arrangement for bringing about the Revolution of 1688. The Dutch experiment of an imported King was a great success. Not so the German; and the unabated prosperity and the unchecked progression of England under the four Georges is a demonstration that the momentum of a great people, at a certain stage of development, is not to be arrested by the incapacity of kings, and that England has outgrown kingship. Kingship has ceased to be an inward need of the nation. England continues yet for a while to keep it, as an ornamental externality, a cherished national heirloom sparkling with historic prestige, a time-blazoned emblem of majesty, a conventional centre, to and from which run all the lines of executive routine, just as the parallels of longitude seem to depend on Greenwich, — and because, without the broad certain shade of the crown, the still powerful oligarchy of England would be exposed to the relentless sun of Democracy, which surely burns and blasts all mere hereditary pretensions to power and preëminence.

Through Shrewsbury, Birmingham, Warwick, we came to Stratford-on-Avon. If an area with a circumference so jagged with promontories, so eccentric and desultory, can have a centre, that of England and Wales will probably lie somewhere in Warwickshire, the geographical heart being thus the cradle of the poetic; as though England were so careful and jealous of her foremost man, that she nestled him in her interior precincts; as though she would guard on every side, with all the breadth of land her island could furnish, the sanctuary where was to grow and play the big-eyed boy who, about 1574, began to have inward hints, vague intimations, pulses dimly quivering with that power which was to be one of the strongest and most continuous forces upon the British, and through that upon the whole civilized, mind.

Shakespeare is by much the most creative poet the earth has known. A creative mind is one within whose womb are engendered fresh births, additions of new forms, conceptions, ideas, to the intellectual treasures of humanity. Within it is such a combination and intense concentration of the higher human, that it has the august privilege of overflowing in gifts that enlarge, enrich, fortify, and beautify human kind. The multitude and variety, the splendor and solidity, the originality and beauty, the liveliness and inexhaustible significancy of the thoughts, images, conceptions, personages, added by Shakespeare to the human stock, enthrone him supreme in the saturnian realms of mental creation. In him, more than in any other writer, there is a cumulative vitality — thought breeding thought, so saturated is the soil with parturient seed, so heaving with organic readiness. And what gives such sparkle and proportion to this fertility is the natural order, the essential sequence, of fact and feeling, the fine æsthetic logic, as it may be termed, — thoughts and resolves and mutations following one another according to the subtlest most necessary law. A characteristic of his scenes is an unresting progressiveness. Healthfully, alertly, each movement unfolds itself under the sway of a judgment made intuitive by a deep multiplex life-power. Shoot projects shoot, as all over a vigorous tree in May. Some poets have to cast about for themes, and are at times put to it to fill up their outline: Shakespeare is ever rejecting, and has only to eliminate before enranking his abundance.

A feature, and in its prominence a distinctive feature of Shakespeare, and one whose full import has not been weighed, that I am aware of, is his wealth of metaphor. Some of his best pages are an almost unintermitted roll of metaphor. Abundant, various, fresh metaphor involves full, fine knowledge of the relations among countless things, and implies a rich, far-glancing, and moreover a poetic mind; for it is chiefly by means of metaphor that the poetic imagination, telescopic and telegraphic, flashes new meanings through old words, suddenly fuses into one two things hitherto separate and distant, reveals unexpected similitudes, unnoticed sympathies. Good metaphors bite into the core of things; they glisten with the very sap of substance.

For a wide segment of her annals England has in Shakespeare a unique historiographer. No other people enjoys the privilege of reading its history by the light of poetry; for the Greek tragedies are as unhistoric as are Lear and Macbeth. The Henrys and Richards, with their vizored nobles, Shakespeare uplifts to where they can come within the focus of his illumination. On his page they are the authentic agents imaginatively transfigured; aggrandized, not falsified; only the more real for being seen in the glow of a Shakespearean ideal. His historic dramas are the truth of history exalted.

From Stratford through Shipston we came to Woodstock, stopping at Blenheim to see the old pictures and the old oaks. Of Oxford we had only an outside glimpse, taking but a peep into the Bodleian Library. From Oxford through Henley to London.

Were wishes not often baffled, expectations often disappointed, we should be led to misplace and exaggerate our hopes, and would grow inflated with a temporal prosperity. And, the world being still under the momentum of animal self-seeking energies, to suppose (except that, amid our endless conflicts, this were to suppose a monstrous impossibility) the plans and hopes, personal and ambitious, of every one as to earthly things always gratified, and you turn humanity into a slimy putrid mass of ceaseless, bootless fermentation, a weltering concupiscent shoal wriggling in mud; you convert the earth into a wilderness of Satanic serpents; you make of men mere intellectual beasts. The obstacles to gratification are our safeguards. The grosser the nature the more it owes to its limitations. Through failure and discontent and mortification our spiritual powers are strengthened, to purge and discipline our desires. Trouble is to many a dark glass, through which they are enabled to cast their eyes up to God, whom without it they could not look at, and should not turn their eyes to.

A sentence will suffice to whisk the reader from London to Paris. Tarrying some weeks in Antwerp with my uncle and aunt, who planned the journey in which they were to accompany us, we tarried again in Aix-la-Chapelle, whose baths were recommended to one of our party; and thence up the Rhine, through Switzerland and Lyons, we reached Paris early in the autumn.

Gas had not yet arrived at Paris. Across the streets at the corners and at remote intervals were hung ropes with a lantern in the middle, giving out rays that served for little more than to make the darkness visible. The streets had no sidewalks; the gutters ran in the middle; the boulevards were unpaved; the Madeleine unfinished. With a population of about five hundred thousand, Paris was unsightly and dirty, at night gloomy and forbidding; and in the Tuileries was enthroned Charles X., surrounded with men who undertook to rule a great people without foresight, who had not enough discourse of reason to look before or after, could not even see what the past was or the future might be, and would make of the present a cushion to loll on.

In a former chapter is described a dinner I partook of (with the eyes) in the dining-room of the King of Saxony. To be one of the company where a King of France dines — and he, mark you, the last of the long regal line of the elder

Bourbons — is a feast as much more delicate as finest champagne is than home-brewed perry. Nor were we, as in Saxony, shut into a gallery above, but we passed along beside the royal table, fenced off by a balustrade, and so near that had his Majesty been so minded he could, by means of but two intermediaries, have handed to me (the gentleman in waiting having first refilled it) the capacious glass he was just draining of what, I must believe, was Clos Vougeot of '22. And possibly he might have become so minded, could he by a prophetic flash have read, that the act of unprecedented royal hospitality would be recorded on the present page. The old king (the same who as the young Compte d'Artois the beautiful queen, Marie Antoinette, was charged — unjustly, no doubt — with having too freely flirted with) had an oval face, with forehead and chin somewhat retreating, and a flushed complexion — a countenance without any sparkle in it. We were not allowed to stop, but were urged slowly forward, so that I had but time to receive the image of one other member of the party, which only consisted of three or four, at a table about five feet square. This person stood erect by the side of the table, with her masculine countenance turned toward the moving spectators as if with a suppressed scowl. It was the Duchesse d'Angoulême, designated as the only man of the family. She was superbly dressed, and her pointed stomacher, four or five inches wide, was a glittering field of close-packed diamonds.

The minister of the United States to France was Mr. Brown, of Louisiana, who, having an ample fortune, "lived in handsome style," while his and Mrs. Brown's command of French gave a completeness to the qualifications of the mission and a finish to its hospitalities, seldom attained by American legations on the Continent. At Mr. Brown's I first met Fenimore Cooper, then light of figure, and, sitting next to him at dinner one day, have a pleasant memory of his lively talk. To their minister several young Americans were indebted for an invitation to the grand ball of the season, given at the spacious mansion of one of the notabilities of that and the preceding era, — Pozzo di Borgo, ambassador from Russia, by birth a Corsican, and a life-long persistent hater of, and counterworker against, his countryman, Napoleon. Here was assembled much of the titled population of Paris, resident and transient. My recollections carry only the general brilliant effect, the affable smile of the host, — one of the handsomest men of his day, — the meeting with a fellow-student of Goettingen, *attaché* to the Russian mission, and a portrait of the new Emperor, Nicholas, which hung by itself, over a dais representing the throne, in one of the interior rooms.

M. Hyde de Neuville had recently returned to

Paris from the United States, where for several years he had been minister of France. He and Madame de Neuville being both of the *ancienne noblesse*, and both distinguished specimens of their class, and he a public man in high estimation, at their evening parties, which were frequent, I had an opportunity of superficially seeing the *élite* of that old French nobility, historical and renowned, whose doom had been knelled in shrieking dissonances by the Revolution, and who, come back with the Bourbon throne, were trying to rewarm themselves with fragments of decayed, disrupted institutions, and to rebuild the old monarchic edifice; for, having, in their long obscurity and exile, "learnt nothing and forgotten nothing," they could not perceive that the foundations of their ancient power were destroyed or loosened, and that History had outgrown them. Fixing their eyes on the past, with their backs turned to the future, — reversing the healthful order of nature, — the future came upon them as a sudden hurricane, and in 1830 they were again swept out of the Palace, never more to return to it.

This devotion to and reliance upon the past, which, spiritually speaking, has its source in a religious insufficiency, in a timid moral halfness, afraid of the livelier half, the future that puts us on our mettle, — this indolent spiritual *dolce far niente*, this pauper-piety, that would cower out of the wind behind the high wall of the past, arrogates for its devotees precedence over all other earth-born immortals, the highest place in God's regard; as though a moral and religious passivity were the first of virtues. These excessive Bourbonists were ultra-Romanists. But are not they, and all who like them strive to enthrone and immortalize the past and mistrust the future, the real infidels? The unbeliever is he who dreads and has no faith in what is to come. The reprobate or simpleton can believe in the past. That every one has in possession without effort. But belief in the future demands spiritual activity. Is it not a subtle form of materialism, to fear the future because you know it not? Is not this an impious egotism? What you see and have you believe, but what you cannot see and have not, you trust not God to provide. Much less will you help him to provide it, by tolerance, by enlargement of the area of moral and political freedom, by disinterested wishes and aims, by arduous and helpful wisdom.

We lodged at Meurice's Hotel, not the modern Meurice but the ancient, a hundred yards nearer to the Palais Royal, much less capacious than the new, with the main entrance on the *Rue St. Honoré;* for the arcade of the *Rue Rivoli* was not yet finished so far. It is now, or was some years since, still a public house, under the name of Hotel

Bedford. Our fellow-lodgers were almost exclusively English, and a portion of these, with two or three who took their meals at the hotel, with occasional stragglers, made a circle of twelve or fifteen at the *table-d'hôte;* and my father and I separated ourselves at dinner from the rest of our party for the companionship of the public table, which was not open to ladies. Ere the winter was half over the circle had got kneaded into sociability.

Our most notable member was Colonel Beckwith, of the British army, a man of large merit and little pretension, whose worth and purity of nature were soon apparent through simple manners and amiable openness. He had lost a leg at Waterloo, and one evening he made his amputated limb illustrate a spiritual argument. His leg, buried on the field, was to him no more than the soil wherein it lay, and thus would soon be the rest of his body, was so in a measure already. Having lately returned from travelling in the United States, and speaking of marriage, he remarked, that young Englishmen were often deterred from marrying by the expensive habits of English girls; in this, he added, contrasting strikingly with those of the United States. (American young gentlemen of 1866, shake your heads, ejaculate as stoutly as you please: you were not born when that remark was made, and forty years bring almost unimaginable changes.) His latter days Col. Beckwith spent among the Waldenses, founding schools in their secluded beautiful valleys, — an active benefactor to that heroic fragment of a people.

We had a *ci-devant* dandy among us, an Englishman with a high French title, about thirty-five years of age, who had been an officer in the English "Guards," — amiable, intelligent, handsome, and unaffected, with little left of the dandy except the elegance of his dress. — One of the occasional diners was a man, rather tall, turned of forty, with a thin nose, whose habitual expression was almost uncivil, so soured was it by the acidity of his nature, — a man whom it irked to hear any one, and even any thing, praised, as though thereby he were robbed, — one of those porous egotists who try to absorb all around them into themselves, and move about in the twilight of their semi-illuminated self-busied sensations. — Another, who appeared at long intervals, ten years younger than this one, and to him as a racer to a dray-drudge, had light hair, finely cut Roman features, bloodless complexion, a pale, high, cold forehead, and clear gray eyes, the rays out of which were like the trickle from shining icicles, — a man full of suggestion to a female sensation novelist, — a calm mysterious Voltairian, whose smile was but the play on the surface, of a deep habitual scorn. There was a middle-aged Englishman, settled in Normandy, even fonder than most men of hearing himself talk, especially about his own adventures and doings, one of that class of ambitious overtopping talkers for whose swelling speech God's works and man's are too diminutive, — individuals whose frontal sinus, instead of being empty as in their meaner fellows, carries in it a magnifying lens made of cerebral vapor, — practical transcendentalists, so much do their facts transcend the unbecoming littleness of reality. One day this Anglo-Norman was giving an account of his gardens and plantations, especially of his acres of roses, his hundreds of varieties, his tens of thousands of bushes, his cart-loads of rose-leaves, when, amid interjections of admiration from some of his auditors, he of the pallid brow said, "then you can lie on roses," in a voice so quiet and concurrent that few took the hit — an obtuseness which heightened rather than lowered the zest of the satirist in his stroke.

One young man, with fair skin, blue eyes, and beautiful teeth, which were well seen through a frequent laugh, had a living of six hundred pounds in his family, which they were anxious for him to qualify himself to take; but he had scruples, not feeling in him any vocation for the higher clerical duties — a scrupulousness which, if acted on, would empty many a pulpit in England, and elsewhere. — From another I learnt that a young lady in England was in danger of making a very bad match. My informant was a young man of six or seven and twenty, with round face and head, a smooth ruddy skin over features that would have made him a fine-looking fellow but for his eye, the expression of which was always dubious, and at times deeply sinister. He told me that a girl of his own age, of good position, face, and figure, a neighbor of his in the country, with three hundred a year in possession, was ready to take him whenever he should say the word. He was evidently holding her and her three hundred a year in reserve, as a last resource should he not do better. She had my cordial wishes for escape from one who seemed already entering, with no unsteady step, the dusky downward road of vice.

One day Sir Francis Burdette appeared at the table — a tall, striking man with long face, light hair, and a remarkably high-bred look.

Of eminent Frenchmen then living and since deceased, there is but one whom I much regret not to have seen. It is not Chateaubriand; for he was only one of the most splendid of rhetoricians, who, chiefly through gifts of expression, became, without being wise or truly commanding, a power among his contemporaries, and not always a power for good.

The man whose face and voice I should now delight to be able to recall, and whom, could I have then dreamt what he would become to me,

I might easily have seen, — he being that very winter a clerk in the American house of Curtis and Lamb in Paris, — was Charles Fourier, just then busy with his *Nouveau Monde Industriel et Sociétaire*, "New Industrial and Social World," a volume of five hundred pages, an abridgment of his large cardinal work in four volumes, entitled *Théorie de l'Unité Universelle.*

A profound thinker, whose thinking moved in broad, disinterested channels, Fourier outran his fellow-men by several generations, and through intuitions that had their germs in enlarged humanity and noble love of justice, discovered, by dint of arduous meditative endeavor, the laws of work, whereby all human industry, by being organized and thereby purified and made attractive, shall quadruple its products, and the discords of selfish, ruthless competition and perverted passion be harmonized, — laws whose easy power lies in the multitudinous capacities and boundless resources and scientific thirst of the human mind, ever longing for a higher method, — laws benignant and beautiful, that were brought to light by the piercing insight of genius and sympathy.

But it is time to bring the chapter, and the volume, to a close. Early in the spring of 1827 we passed over to London, and in May sailed from Liverpool in an American packet for Philadelphia.

THE END.

www.ingramcontent.com/pod-product-compliance
Lightning Source LLC
LaVergne TN
LVHW020233110826
845151LV00003B/907

* 9 7 8 1 4 2 5 5 3 0 6 5 5 *